LIVE COURAGEOUSLY

LIVE COURAGEOUSLY

Choose to Be the Real You

Revelations From the Life of a Stuntwoman

TERRI CADIENTE

DESTINY IMAGE® PUBLISHERS, INC.
P.O. Box 310, Shippensburg, PA 17257-0310

"Speaking to the Purposes of God for this Generation and for the Generations to Come."

This book and all other Destiny Image, Revival Press, Mercy Place, Fresh Bread, Destiny Image Fiction, and Treasure House books are available at Christian bookstores and distributors worldwide.

For a U.S. bookstore nearest you, call **1-800-722-6774.**

For more information on foreign distributors, call **717-532-3040.**

Or reach us on the Internet: **www.destinyimage.com**

ISBN 10: 0-7684-2820-3

ISBN 13: 978-0-7684-2820-9

For Worldwide Distribution, Printed in the U.S.A.

1 2 3 4 5 6 7 8 9 10 11 / 13 12 11 10 09

DEDICATION

This book is a reflection of what is possible when a life is restored and a heart is healed. If anything praiseworthy is found, whatever I am, it is all because of the kindness and mercy poured out upon my life.

ACKNOWLEDGMENTS

God, without Your Love, these are simply words on paper; I am grateful.

Jeff, thank you for your gracious presence in my life. Tiffany, where are those wings? Jasmyn and Jolie, you are strength and grace. Mom, "They will return to their borders." Unc, you are a genius! Dr. Mark Chironna, I am forever changed by your coaching and mentoring. Graham and Laurie, you bring out the best in me. Don, thank you for taking time with me. Pamela and Richard, thank you for seeing me and loving me. Donna, *now* it makes sense; could not have done it without you! Rene, my voice is grateful to you. Dianne—what a speaking coach! Thank you, my friends, for your unconditional love.

To my stunt-sista's—the most beautiful women who have the heart to take it to the wall and through the fire— you will emerge like gold. I admire your gifts and talents.

ENDORSEMENTS

I met Terri approximately twenty years ago. Her accomplishments are many. She actually presented to me her gold medal in jet skiing as a token of appreciation for my investment into her life through my ministry. It was a cherished moment in front of hundreds of people. Since that time, Terri has risen above the setbacks, the discouragements, the ups and the downs of a very busy career, to become a woman of love, grace, and freedom.

I highly recommend the assimilation of the contents of this book. Not so much because it's a good read, but that it is the journey of truth. And...it is *truth* that sets us free. Happy journey!

—Glen D. Cole, Senior Pastor
Trinity Life Center
Sacramento, California

Pastor Emeritus, Capital Christian Center
Sacramento, California
Superintendent Emeritus, Assemblies of God
Northern California/Nevada District Council

Terri Cadiente has a unique perspective in her new book *Live Courageously*...unique because it contains her journey and her total life experience. If we are going to change lives, then it is imperative that we become authentic, transparent, and genuinely open about where we have been and what we have endured. We all hide behind masks of our own making in hopes that no one will see through the mask to the pain we bury beneath it. Yet, the key to real, lasting freedom and joy is the unmasking of the pain and the honesty it takes to deeply and profoundly accept ourselves with all our weaknesses and limitations and then walk in total unconditional acceptance and find our limitless and boundless destiny unfold. Read the entire treatise and apply the life lessons and become all you can be. Terri is an amazing woman who has accomplished far more than most in her life, and I am honored to have her as a friend and to have spent some time coaching her on her road to exquisite destiny.

—Dr. Mark J. Chironna
Orlando, Florida

The idea of people reaching their dreams is a particularly powerful one. True to form, Terri shows us that it is possible to achieve your dreams by striking the balance of strength and grace. Soroptimist International of the America's *Live Your Dream Campaign* focuses on raising awareness about the unique challenges women face and ways that they can be supported in their quest to live their dreams.

—Leigh Wintz, CAE
Executive Director
Soroptimist International of the Americas
www.soroptimist.org
www.liveyourdreamcampaign.org

As a mother raising three girls, a career as a recording artist, the wife of an NFL giant, and simply being a woman, there are always opportunities to play the field in a "role."

In this book and real life, Terri will challenge you to your best game and show you how to *not* "size down or dumb down," but instead, to face your fears, and stand up in your own identity, refusing the cheap imitation of an image as something to be pursued or obtained.

—Sevyn Lindsay
(a.k.a., Mrs. Marshall Faulk).

I have had the pleasure and honor of knowing Terri Cadiente for more than 20 years, and I am proud to be her friend. Her heart and her kindness have always been self-evident, character traits made even more impressive by the fact that Terri has been respected and sought after in the rough and tumble, thick-skinned world of motion picture stunts. I have always been impressed that her bravery, skill, and enthusiasm to perform death-defying stunts have always gone hand in hand with a bubbly, warm, and caring personality. Terri is truly a hyphenate of the highest order.

—Lou Diamond Phillips
Actor

Terri Cadiente is a phoenix that has risen from the ashes of veritable adversity and is a force of love and inspiration to the human race. For those who are ready to stop making excuses from fear and choose to actively live a life of freedom, I highly recommend this book. What Terri has accomplished within herself and how she guides us is an inspiration. After reading *Live Courageously,* I am acting on the disguised awareness that I kept pushed down for fear of failing, and I have come to understand and embrace the reality that the human spirit can overcome any adversity.

—Krista Allen
Actress, single mother, artist

TABLE OF CONTENTS

Foreword 15

Preface 17

Chapter 1   The Hiding Place 23

Chapter 2   Check Your Gait 35

Chapter 3   Caught on Tape 55

Chapter 4   Shatter Your Invisible Wheelchair 73

Chapter 5   Unmask Your Authentic Identity 89

Chapter 6   Choice—The Power of Your C.A.R. 107

Chapter 7   Action Puts Your C.A.R. in Motion 123

Chapter 8   Ride Your C.A.R. to Rewarding Results 139

Chapter 9   Take the Edge—Launch Your Biggest Life! 157

Chapter 10 Experience Transformation:
            From Invisible to Transparent 177

Chapter 11   Reframe Your Foundation in 10 Dynamic Days:
              Days 1–5 195

Chapter 12   Reframe Your Foundation in 10 Dynamic Days:
              Days 6–10 213

Conclusion   You Are an Absolute Wonder! 229

              Endnotes 243

FOREWORD

AS the years have gone by, I have watched as Terri has refused to rest on her laurels and has expanded her personal challenges far beyond the realm of the movie set. She has become a wonderful wife and mother and as if that weren't enough, has become a strong and vibrant voice for community service and social change, never hesitating to be a soldier for those less fortunate than herself. She has faced every challenge with optimism, infectious enthusiasm, and a deep-seated faith in herself and a Higher Power. Terri is certainly one of those people who has made the world and the people whose lives she has touched better for her presence.

I am, therefore, not surprised that Terri has decided to share her experience and gathered wisdom in a book. Once again, Terri Cadiente has expanded her horizons and is leading by example, not only for those in her immediate sphere, but now, to a much larger audience. I'm sure that the life she has led will prove to be insightful, helpful, and life affirming for those who read her words and have a chance to experience Terri's generosity like I and so many of her friends have done for years.

—Lou Diamond Phillips

PREFACE

"People grow through experience if they meet life honestly and courageously.
This is how character is built."
—Eleanor Roosevelt

ELEANOR Roosevelt's words are more than empty musings written by a speech writer for the first lady. They capture the conviction of a remarkable woman who experienced their truth. Eleanor Roosevelt was a strong woman who endured painful losses, often in plain view of the public. Still, she persevered—through her husband's battle with polio, his betrayal of their marriage through infidelity, and even the death of their infant son.

Can you relate to Mrs. Roosevelt?

Most every person who holds this book can honestly say, "Yes; I have experienced loss." In one way or another, *each of us* has experienced life's bumps and bruises. Some can point to a less-than-perfect childhood, a life filled with setbacks and rejection, and the deep emotional wounds that resulted.

As a Hollywood stuntwoman, I am familiar with bumps and bruises. I take them on purpose, and it's never pretty. I'm required to leap tall buildings in a single bound (no cape required), and even when I don't land well, I'm expected to get up for the next take. I perch on the tops of cars that are spinning out of control, stand next to things that explode, and allow myself to be caught in fires and floods. After a day's work, it's my job to brush myself off and prepare for the next gig.

Parallels between stunt work and "real" life aside, it can take much longer to bounce back from the emotional injuries each of us sustains. These wounds often fly under the radar, going unnoticed or ignored. Yet, uncared-for emotional wounds that fester out of conscious sight can produce a lifetime of unintended, unrecognized consequences and cause us to live far below our potential.

This is a lesson I learned the hard way, through many years of painful experiences. Today, with 20/20 hindsight, I realize that even as a child who was strong in mind and body, I was not immune to emotional woundedness—and even the strongest woman cannot power her way to healing.

Where did my bumps and bruises come from? The place where most hurts have their beginning: in childhood. As a child with a vibrant personality and big ideas, I didn't fit into the box or conform to the definition that others had for me. Without knowing it, I broke their unspoken rules and crossed an invisible emotional boundary.

Until the moment I collided head-on with those rules, I was blissfully ignorant of their existence. Yet, I soon discovered the stiff penalty for rule-breaking—rejection!

Today I would liken that experience to attempting a stunt without understanding the science involved—and then trying to do it blindfolded. Once stuff starts exploding, it's too late to protect yourself. You're caught off-guard, unprepared, and vulnerable.

Children—even strong ones—are by nature vulnerable to suggestion. They easily discern and internalize the signs of rejection, however subtle those signs may be. This was certainly true in my case. I recognized my loved ones' disapproval, and I absorbed the impact of their rejection. As a result, I placed a negative value on my own self-worth and spent decades trying to perform my way to acceptance.

Rejection hurts more deeply than being catapulted from a speeding car on a movie set. Still, much as I do in my stunt work today, I had to find a way to brush myself off and face another day. My childhood method of coping was not to fight back, but to formulate a safer, "smaller" version of myself—a persona that didn't rock anybody else's boat.

What I was really doing was *hiding*. I shrank myself down to a size that was more acceptable to others and then safely tucked the real me out of their sight.

Although hiding enabled me to please and gain the acceptance of others, over time it produced deep emotional problems. I was caught in an endless cycle of performance and behavior that satisfied my addiction for approval but left me feeling unfulfilled and dishonest.

To gain affirmation, I traded away my identity! That's the steep price of an approval addiction. I became a derivative of myself, carefully calibrated to elicit positive feedback from those around me. However, the approval I received was not for the real me. It was for the person I had fabricated; so instead of feeling reassured, I felt ashamed.

As is true of all deceptive practices, over time I had to drill down deeper and deeper to maintain my cover-up. I had to raise protective "shields"—identities laced with attraction and power—behind which I could hide my broken self-image.

One of my shields was my profession. Most people have never met a stunt-person and are taken with the mystique of the business. They can't imagine doing the things I do for a living; so the title of *stuntwoman* projects power. For years it served as a dazzling calling card that spoke highly of me to others because it said:

Terri is strong;

Terri is fearless;

Terri is unique and sought after.

The attraction of others to my stuntwoman persona was wildly affirming to me. It mollified my sense of powerlessness and shored up my fragile sense of identity—not with substance, but with image. It made me feel less broken, if only for a moment.

The affirmation received as a result of my job title blurred the lines between my genuine and false identities. It downgraded the importance of *who I am* on the inside and drew attention to the one-dimensional measure of *what I do*. Since performance was the only measure of my human value, every less-than-perfect outcome dug a deeper emotional hole and further slashed my self-worth.

The hiding place I had created was anything but safe! My performance mentality became a slippery slope where every misstep forced me to compensate by performing next time at even higher levels. The higher the bar was set, the more imminent failure became and the harder I had to work to perform flawlessly.

Today, performance plays a much healthier role in my life. By God's grace I am strong in body and mind and skilled in my profession. A dangerous stunt is no longer an identity booster or an adrenaline fix—*it's my job*. My contribution to the filmmaking process is to ensure that thrilling scenes make it to the big screen without anyone getting hurt, including me.

When I'm about to perform a stunt, I know by experience and study what to expect. Every possible precaution is taken to protect those involved. The stunt is choreographed, and protective gear is put in place. Everything the stunt crew and I know about the science of stunt work is taken into consideration. We create and control chaos to produce spectacular effects. The effect is limited, and the outcome is predetermined.

Although real life can be equally dramatic, it is never as controlled or predictable as one of my stunts. Your story may resemble mine. Perhaps your childhood simply *happened* and you found yourself in the midst of situations and outcomes for which you were unprepared. With neither safety gear nor the power to affect the choices of others, you absorbed the impact of the dysfunctional actions of others and sustained unnecessary emotional injuries.

Injuries do not heal overnight—not for you; not for me; not for Eleanor Roosevelt. Yet, *they can heal,* and your life can start afresh! You can come out of hiding forever *if* you are willing to be transparent (with yourself first of all). and if you desire to become the authentic *you* the Creator designed you to be.

Eleanor Roosevelt was right: honesty and courage can turn a bad situation into an opportunity for growth. Get downright honest with yourself. Be courageous by confronting the lies that have held you captive and replace them with the truth that you were wonderfully, exquisitely created to be you.

Are you ready to live free in the present?

Will you allow yourself to put the past to rest?

Are you determined to begin moving in the direction of your desired outcomes?

Is the voice in your heart inviting you out of hiding and urging you forward into your hopes, desires, and dreams?

Don't allow fear to talk you out of it. Freedom to be the real *you*, the authentic you, your biggest self, is what you were designed for. This book is your invitation—you could think of it as your "get out of jail free card." It could be your best opportunity to leave behind the things that limit you and walk into your destiny.

Will you seize the moment? Will you give yourself permission to accept this invitation and begin the amazing adventure of rediscovering and becoming your genuine self?

Chapter 1

THE HIDING PLACE

NOW middle-aged and alone, Lieutenant Hiroo Onoda had been hiding in the dangerous jungle of Lubang Island since he was twenty years old. Although he looked tattered in his soiled and ragged clothing, he was alert to danger and prepared for war. He meticulously maintained his Type 99 Japanese-issue Arisaka rifle, keeping it in pristine working condition, just as he had since first arriving on this Philippine island in 1944.

Unaware of Japan's surrender on August 14, 1945, Onoda and his Japanese comrades lived in survival mode and continued to wage war for more than twenty-five years. Fiercely loyal to their country, they clung to their commander's final orders to *never* give up their lives voluntarily, and to wait patiently, for as long as necessary, until returning Japanese forces came to their rescue.

The men lived on coconuts and bananas and the occasional snared bird or stolen cow. Unafraid to use their well-kept weapons, they continued the war, fighting with every ounce of their strength. Believing themselves to be Japan's defenders, they killed no fewer than thirty Filipinos assumed to be spies or enemy combatants coming to take them prisoner and shame their nation.

Year after year, these fierce warriors avoided capture...and unwittingly rejected freedom. When search parties and American B-17s dropped leaflets in an attempt to persuade them that the war was over, the soldiers hunkered down, convinced the message was a ploy of the enemy to capture or kill them.

When the Japanese survivors on Lubang Island spotted innocent islanders nearby, they maintained their cover, certain the civilians were actually enemy spies. And when the voices of Onoda's own heartbroken family members echoed through the jungle over loudspeakers, imploring him to come out and recognize the war's end, the lieutenant's resolve was only strengthened. Onoda and his men refused to be tricked into surrender; they were determined to protect themselves and their country's honor—if necessary, to the death.

By 1974, the jungle had taken its toll: Onoda's youth was spent, and all of his comrades were dead. Although his country and the world had long since emerged from the shadows of World War II, Onoda remained focused on a mission that had long since ended—and on an enemy who no longer existed. Although he had upheld his nation's cause at great personal cost, his years of sacrifice would prove pointless.

In an instant, Onoda's life would be turned upside down. His hiding place would be stripped of its meaning, and freedom, which had come calling so many times before, would be thrust upon the unsuspecting warrior in the form of a startling new reality.

Onoda's paradigm shift began when Noria Suzuki, a young Japanese student, came to Lubang Island looking for him. Suzuki coaxed the lieutenant out of hiding and arranged for Onoda's former commander to return to the jungle and announce the war's end.

On March 9, 1974, Major Taniguchi, the only person Onoda believed he could trust, read aloud the orders to cease all combat activity. After almost 30 years, Onoda's long-awaited rescue had come, but with an unwelcome dose of reality—the shocking news that Japan had suffered defeat at the hands of her enemies.

Onoda grappled with his new reality and as the truth set in, a wave of emotion—a torrent of rage—washed over him. Onoda realized that his 30 years of meager existence in a dangerous environment had been a waste of time. His complete dedication to a single mission had been *for nothing*!

> Suddenly everything went black. A storm raged inside me. I felt like a fool for having been so tense and cautious on the way [to the meeting with Taniguchi]. Worse than that, what had I been doing for all these years?...I pulled back the bolt on my rifle and unloaded the bullets....I eased off the pack that I always carried with me and laid the gun on top of it. Would I really have no more use for this rifle that I had polished and cared for like a baby all these years?[1]

Liberation brought a rude awakening to Lieutenant Onoda...the realization that all of his decisions over the past 30 years, made in obedience to authority and with the best of intentions, had actually been a terrible mistake. His misadventure had not only cost Onoda the prime of his life—it had also brought death to the innocents who had crossed his path.

Stunned, the lieutenant realized that he had inadvertently sentenced himself to a life cut off from his dreams...all because of a *misunderstanding*.

My story is not as dramatic as Lieutenant Onoda's, yet a day came when I, too, discovered that I had created for myself a small, unfulfilling life based upon a misunderstanding. Is it possible that you, too, have banished yourself to mere existence? Has a misunderstanding limited your happiness and held you back from becoming all you could be and having all you could have?

THE SCARS OF BATTLE...THE LURE OF THE HIDING PLACE

Before atomic bombs were dropped on Hiroshima and Nagasaki, Onoda's choices made perfect sense. His survival was remarkable, yet his life was meant to be much more than a game of hide and seek in a steamy, dangerous jungle. Lubang Island should have been a passing experience, not Onoda's ultimate destiny. A much fuller life beckoned to him over the decades, but until he was ready to accept new information and leave the war behind, he continued to hide...*from nothing.*

Onoda's story is extreme, yet there are aspects of his experience to which each of us can relate. Like him, we can become so fully invested in our perceptions, in the things we have been told, and the painful things we have come to believe about ourselves, that we long to hide. We can erect iron-clad defenses against our universal enemies—*fear, shame, rejection, loss of identity, disappointment, abandonment,* or *insecurity.*

If we're completely honest with ourselves, we know this to be true: Every one of us is hiding from something. All of us, at least intermittently, fear that our frailties will be exposed, that we might not measure up, and that we might be cast aside.

This sense of insecurity can cause us to forfeit the very things we desire most, because in order to remain safe, we often opt for self-limiting behaviors, such as the following:

- We prevent failure by withdrawing from the very opportunities that could give us what we want

- We become so preoccupied with self-protection that we lack the energy to pursue our dreams

- We avoid rejection and abandonment by sacrificing the very thing we desire in our relationships, which is intimacy.

As members of the human race, all of us qualify us for some level of insecurity, so don't be afraid to own up to yours. You may relate to one or more of the examples of insecurity-driven behavior listed above. Or as you read on, you could be recognizing some issues for the very first time.

Whether your name is Onoda or Smith, life sometimes feels like war. Sadly, the wounds suffered in life's battles often go unhealed. Depending upon the injured warrior's state of mind and approach to life, these wounds will either serve as evidence of human resilience or will serve as anchors to keep emotions fixed in the past.

It is not my intention to discredit the battles you have faced or discount the level of emotion your war required. Perhaps you can look back to a memorable skirmish and say without hesitation, "I was absolutely right in my assessment of the situation. I took the actions the crisis demanded."

Yet, whatever your opinion of your past responses may be, the questions you face today are simple:

With eyes wide open regarding the events of the past, are you ready to move on?

How important is it for you to be proven right in regard to an old issue?

Do you value being right more than you value the need to grow in the present?

When all is said and done, will you forfeit the good life that is ahead in order to cling, as Lieutenant Onoda did, to the alienation, isolation, misunderstanding, and deprivation your war has produced?

We can easily misread reality and exile ourselves to Lubang Islands of our own choosing. Hidden there, we have little to do but keep our weapons polished, raise defensive shields against future attacks, and watch as the world moves forward without us.

Instead of assigning our negative experiences to their appropriate place *in history*, we can limp under their back-breaking burden and live lives weighed down with pain. Unaware that the war is actually over, we can carry our undressed wounds into hiding places where they will never see the light of day—and conceal them in the darkness, where they can never heal.

CREATE THE BOUNCE

I've mentioned my work as a Hollywood stuntwoman. I wear a second professional hat in my work as a life coach.

On the movie set, I step in to complete action scenes for the star of the movie. In this role, I essentially operate undercover. In my role as life coach, I work with clients who want to come out from under their emotional cover (including old baggage, lingering issues, and painful memories) to live more fruitful, satisfying lives.

When working with clients, I use verbal cues in the form of language that supports *positive motion* or movement in a constructive direction. One such expression is *create the bounce*. This phrase helps us to open a dialogue in the areas of attitude and choice.

Without the fear or risk of being judged, clients can take an honest look at their attitudes and evaluate their choices. By assessing these choices, clients can determine whether their proposed actions are something they have tried before—whether it has produced the desired results—or whether they want to make room in their thinking for an entirely new choice.

On a practical level, to *create the bounce* is to...

- Become aware of the negative and erroneous beliefs driving your thought life

- Form sound beliefs based upon truth that line up with your desired outcomes

- Take actions founded on those sound beliefs.

The negative beliefs we hold on to become running scripts that play insidious messages over and over again in our minds. They are like uninvited Internet programs that operate in the background while you are online; they steal your bandwidth and sabotage your efforts to accomplish something worthwhile. Although you're not consciously aware of these programs working behind the scenes, they drain precious power and diminish overall performance.

As we introduce new concepts throughout this book, you will have interactive opportunities to take what you have discovered and *create the bounce,* using these concepts to create for yourself a better life.

A word of encouragement: In your eagerness to move on and learn the next concept, you may be tempted to skip these opportunities to make personal application. Resist the urge! Applying what you learn *when you learn it* is catalytic. It is the difference between merely *hearing something good* and actually *benefiting from it.*

Application is where real-life progress is made!

CREATE THE BOUNCE

You have reached a potentially transformational moment! Right now you can set in motion a series of positive changes in your life. If you're determined to experience freedom, consider the next few moments as time well spent. Grab a cup of coffee if you like, but leave your Blackberry and other distractions in another room.

Below is an important question for you to ask yourself. Realize that it is completely safe for you to answer honestly. Ducking the question or avoiding the answer only guarantees that you will have the same negative program running in the background of your mind tomorrow— with the same results it has produced in your life so far.

Here's the question: What is the fear that underpins my greatest insecurity and in what ways has my life been governed by it?

As a teen I could not face who I was,— my face, my school work, I dropped out of life — I could not face the drug scene so I rejected them, my life, the world. One break down after another, encouraged to quit High School by my home room teacher. So I did not graduate. More shame. No direction no purpose in life, I wanted more than anything to be a wife and a Mother.

I fell in love, married had two wonderful children and a very verbally abusive m.i.l. I again spiralled downward. Basically I have felt as if I'm catching up for all the lost years afraid I've missed my life's purpose.

Good job! You have taken a giant step, because thoughts are the building blocks of our lives. Now, create the bounce by reassessing your fear and asking yourself, "Is this fear still valid, still warranted?"

In the space provided below, write down some new, more productive ways to respond to this fear and the feelings of insecurity it produces.

Time-management. I have been late for church + have felt shamed, condemned, criticized. I get so anxious + upset that I end up being late.

I have been unmercifully hounded + criticized by Celine, B., M., but strangely enough church is the one I have the most stress with.

? God help?? I am doing better I need more ideas on how I can be on time + stick with "planned neglect" I really need my quiet time + need to plan better things I can do a head of time to improve my prep time + still have "loads of time" for prayer + reflection, 31 I need to forgive myself for feeling a "failure" in this area of my life — my "limp"

I need to forgive all those who harshly criticized me + believe the best for them + believe that I can + will be successful in this area

RETURN TO REAL LIVING

Although few people have a life story as extreme as Lieutenant Onoda's, many of us are emotionally detached from the present, voluntarily suspended in another time. Much as the faithful lieutenant was during his years of exile, we may be in hiding places or *prisons* of our own making, living as though we were captives *to someone* or *something* of which no one else seems to be aware. We may be waiting all too patiently for the "all clear" to be announced so that *someday*, when the danger is over, we can begin living our lives in earnest.

Is that how you feel?

If so, then you are not alone! This may seem shocking, but I have found that most people's lives are on "emotional hold" to some degree, and many of them are unaware that they are stuck in the past.

Not long ago, I was a solid member of that group. I listened attentively to the feedback I received as a child. From my perceptions of that feedback, I created my unique script for life! It became my "gospel"—a set of marching orders that directed every step. I diligently upheld those "orders," much as Lieutenant Onoda did. I took cover on my own Lubang Island and resigned myself to a stifling space where I continually polished my weapon and rehearsed my role:

This is your life: You are confined to this dangerous jungle and your mission is to remain undetected. Keep a low profile; squeeze yourself into your hiding place. Never leave behind signs of your true identity—not a fingerprint, heartbeat, or footprint to point to the authentic you—or you will suffer the consequences: disapproval, rejection, and even abandonment.

Speak only when you're spoken to and others will be more comfortable with you. Don't mention your sense of destiny. Dreamers are not welcome here—and where will you go if you lose your hiding place?

As Lieutenant Onoda had done so many years ago, I took my orders to heart and placed a demand upon my willpower, day after day, to follow to the letter somebody else's flawed directives for my life.

Eventually, I realized that, because I sought the approval of others above all else, I had by default chosen a life of emotional exile, or *hiding*. However, there came a day when hiding was no longer my priority. On that day, I forsook my small island of artificial security so that I could stand up and embrace life in all its fullness. Yes, it is a life filled with risks, but it is also a life brimming with rewards.

Instead of craving acceptance, I began to value my unique identity. As I did so, my life began to change, and I rode that change all the way to freedom. My life did not become perfect; it became *alive*. My wounds did not vanish in an instant, because it takes time for the bumps and bruises to go away. But my days of hiding were over! Regardless of my imperfections, I was heading out of Lubang Island with the voice of liberty resonating in my heart.

Yes, the choice to live an authentic life brings challenges...and the commitment it requires is without parallel. Although hiding will cost you in the long run, it requires less effort in the here and now. On the other hand, the strength produced by this kind of commitment endures. It's resilient; it won't flee or crack when you need it. It will serve you all the days of your life. Without question, the rewards of living an authentic life far outweigh the risks.

Regardless of who or what placed you on Lubang Island, you can leave as a free woman (or man). Yes, you can leave *today!* Abandon your hiding place, battle plans and all. Break free of the lies that have held you down. Become the vibrant, bold, fully functional, and fully empowered person you were created to be. You've already come a long way...and the walk to freedom is not as far as you think.

Chapter 2

CHECK YOUR GAIT

O N the movie set, everyone works hard to create for the audience a sense of reality...a story the viewer can buy into hook, line, and sinker. My job as a stuntperson is to step into the shoes of the character and complete action scenes the way she would have. To accomplish this successfully requires an artful approach. My appearance must be altered, and I must carry myself in such a way as to create the effect that I am the same person who has been onscreen all along.

Watching a great actor at work is stunning to me. What an experience it is to see a pro fully inhabit the role, scene in and scene out. Think about the film actors whose performances have transported you into another reality. In order to make the scene believable, they used every technique and resource at their disposal—body language, tone of voice, facial expression, even personal experience—to bring the story to life and elicit from you sincere pathos for the characters they are playing.

John Wayne is one of those actors. He filled up the screen in such a way that, no matter the role, moviegoers wanted to see him play it. When you hear his name, what comes to mind? Piercing blue eyes? Commanding voice? Towering appearance? Powerful personality?

For many people, one of John Wayne's most outstanding features was his trademark walk...his manly *gait*...his supremely confident way of moving.

According to Merriam-Webster, *gait* is "a manner of walking or moving on foot...a manner or rate of movement or progress."[1] John Wayne's gait was as much a part of his public persona as any other feature for which he was known. Every impersonator worth his salt knew that, to imitate John Wayne, you had to master the actor's distinctive swagger.

When John Wayne burst through bat-winged doors into a Wild West saloon full of bad guys, his bearing spoke volumes—even before he uttered a word. His gait said...

I am in control.

I am not afraid.

I'm a formidable opponent.

I can be relied upon.

I play to win.

I'm a "decider."

John Wayne wasn't known for playing weak characters in need of rescue or uncertain people requiring reassurance. No! He portrayed catalytic personalities, men who could turn bad situations and bad people around by simply walking into a room.

FIRST IMPRESSIONS—YOU ONLY GET ONE CHANCE

Whether your image ever graces the big screen, your gait is one of the first things others notice about you. Every time you walk into a room, others judge *you*, whether consciously or unconsciously, by the way you carry yourself. In that instant when first impressions are formed, your stride reveals who you are and answers the questions they are asking at a subconscious level. Your entrance tells them whether you are:

- Confident

- Self-conscious

- Successful

- Shy

- Fearful

- Strong

- Able to lead

When others meet you for the first time, the question is not *whether* you will make an impression, but *which* impression you will make.

Taking this line of reasoning to its logical conclusion (while bearing in mind that there are always exceptions to every rule), your physical gait can affect outcomes in your life in ways you may never have considered. A desired position could go to someone else simply because your gait gives the impression that you are passive, indecisive, or tentative in your approach. A blind date could end in disappointment because your slouching posture says, "I'm not valuable," leading your date to assume that you are not the companion he or she is seeking.

Although our fictitious interviewer and blind date could have issues of his or her own that skew the dynamics of these imaginary encounters, the fact remains: your gait telegraphs information that others use (often unconsciously) to form an opinion of who you *really* are.

HOW'S YOUR STRIDE ON THE *INSIDE?*

There are exceptions to every rule. Some of the world's most successful and influential people walk in quirky ways that seem inconsistent with their level of accomplishment. Conversely, some very convincing "strutters" mask their insecurity with large doses of practiced body language. As impressive as John Wayne was on the big screen, he surely wasn't immune to human foibles and feelings of insecurity.

Sauntering across the room like a movie star will not guarantee you a lifetime of success and fulfillment any more than waddling like a duck will make you quack like one. The manner in which you walk can be totally unrelated to the person you are on the inside.

But what if the you on the inside is limping?

You may have heard the story of a group of slaves who were freed by a kindly traveler. The man found the slaves confined and in a terrible state, bound at the ankles by heavy shackles and restricted to a very limited area. Determined to see them set free, the man removed their shackles and went on his way.

Sometime later, the traveler returned to the place where the once-shackled slaves had been tethered. He was surprised to discover that the men had remained just where he left them. They had never ventured beyond the place of their former imprisonment—and they continued to limp even though the iron shackles that once weighed them down had been removed.

Although they were no longer physically restricted, the former slaves remained in their small area because they were confined not by leg irons, but by an attitude. Within their minds and hearts, they still saw themselves as slaves. Although their reality had changed and the season of their captivity had ended, the mindset of slavery continued to govern their choices and behavior.

You've heard the oft-repeated axioms:

Attitude is everything.

Your attitude determines your altitude.

Although attitude may not be everything, it certainly comes close. More than any other factor, your attitude about yourself determines how high and how far you will go in life.

Without exception, your attitude will affect every aspect of your life. In a very practical sense, attitude not only affects your external bearing, it is also the emotional backbone that determines your internal posture.

When your attitude is twisted, the rest of your being is forced out of joint. Reactions are skewed, relationships suffer, career is affected, decision-making is compromised, physical and emotional health can deteriorate, and promising opportunities can be lost forever.

Your emotional backbone—your attitude—determines whether you adopt a misshapen posture of *pain* (what is commonly known as a victim mentality) or stand erect in a posture of *power* (a victor's mindset). This internal posture is almost always reflected in your physical bearing, which goes silently before you, as a kind of advance man advertising exactly who you believe yourself to be.

We will tackle attitude in greater detail later on, but it is important for now to bear in mind that, although your attitude may not be visible in the physical sense, *it is always communicated*.

EMOTIONAL BLIND SPOTS AFFECT YOUR GAIT

Have you ever attempted to change lanes on the highway and discovered with alarm that, although you saw no vehicles in your side-view mirror, one was rapidly approaching or had pulled up right beside you? The seemingly invisible car was hidden in your blind spot, the tricky place where the mirror's angle of reflection could not pick up the image of the approaching vehicle.

Emotionally speaking, each of us has blind spots—gaps in perception that prevent us from seeing our world objectively. These blank places on our emotional radar screen result from the woundedness and numbness of unresolved pain.

Blind spots also provide a safe haven for the self-defeating attitudes that form around our wounds. Blind spots keep these attitudes protected from our view; consequently, they become resistant to change and keep us living in a state of involuntary denial. Simply put, as long as self-defeating attitudes remain hidden, we continue to limp.

You may remember a series of television commercials that aired some time ago in which people engaged in important cell phone conversations experienced the awkwardness of having their calls dropped. In each case, the abrupt silence occurred at a critical point in the exchange and was misinterpreted as an unfavorable response.

Emotional blind spots have a similar effect: they cause key pieces of information to "drop out" from our understanding. These blind spots work much like photographic filters do. When filters are used in photography, certain colors are masked, causing a dramatic change in the visual impact of the image. When information is filtered out by a mindset based in emotional woundedness, interaction becomes distorted and misunderstandings occur.

For example, if you believe you are unlovable, you will subconsciously filter out (be unable to see) the actions of those who show you authentic love. You may respond to their behavior with distrust and unwittingly sabotage otherwise beneficial relationships. Likewise, if you believe you have to *perform* in order to be loved, you will attempt to solicit love and develop contrived, often unhealthy, behaviors.

It's time to check your gait. Are you limping through life? Have old wounds produced mindsets that keep you shackled to a hurtful yet defining moment in your past?

If you are bound by self-imposed limitations that say:

My life will never change

Others may find success and happiness, but not me

They were right; I'll never amount to anything

I might as well accept my miserable lot in life...

It's time to get free—really free! Free to the point that you can walk away from your former place of pain, imprisonment, and limitation. Free to the point that you can experience life to the full.

Yes! It's time to strengthen your stride and walk (or better yet, run) without a limp.

STRONG PEOPLE DON'T LIMP...DO THEY?

Everyone has hang-ups. Even the strongest among us deal with woundedness and the distorted belief systems that result from emotional injuries of the past. In one way or another, *everyone* limps.

Sometimes self-deprecating jokes or self-destructive behaviors shine a spotlight on our insecurities and our hidden wounds become apparent to others.

But oftentimes, our emotional injuries are not so evident. This is true of those I call "closet limpers." Outwardly, they look good, smell great, and gain the admiration of others—yet they are secretly shackled on the inside.

Instead of dealing with root issues, closet limpers camouflage their pain by relying on a variety of coping behaviors. They work hard—very hard—to pull themselves together into a seemingly flawless package. They may even learn how to wow others and perform in ways that elicit affirmation. Yet, they are reaching outside themselves to gain a sense of significance and using their abilities, gifts, looks, and talents to gain the approval of others.

For example, a fear of lack can drive an insecure person to become highly successful. The fear of rejection can motivate others to be funny and popular, the quintessential life of the party. Those who were labeled ugly ducklings early in life can become compulsive about fitness or their appearance; multiple surgical enhancements can bear witness to this kind of emotional wound.

My life once served as a vivid example of closet limping. Inside, I was broken, really broken. I saw myself as weak and insignificant. In my mind, I was a ragdoll easily tossed aside and routinely forgotten by others.

Yet the snapshot of Terri that I presented to the outside world projected an image that was quite the opposite. My athleticism provided an external cover-up, an image of strength that concealed the ragdoll within.

Before my days as a stuntwoman, I was a jet-ski racer for *Team Kawasaki*. I used my physical strength and my athletic ability to drive a stake into the heart of my ragdoll image. I established the world record in slalom jet-ski racing—a record that remains unbroken to this day.

We'll talk more about this later; for now, my point is this: things are not always as they seem. You may dazzle people daily with the number of plates you can keep spinning at one time; you may even amaze yourself with your feats of daring. Yet, your stellar performance is not an indication that everything is OK on the inside.

Another important note: Not everyone who desires to succeed, to be well-received, or to maintain an attractive appearance is acting out of his or her pain. However, if you are emotionally wounded, discovering the areas in which you are most driven can help you to pinpoint those emotional wounds.

Whether a limp is painfully obvious or plastered over by compensating behaviors, it is a symptom of what is going on inside. It reveals the condition of your heart, soul, and spirit. It discloses the person you are—or believe yourself to be—on the inside.

The Crippling Cost of Favoring Your Injury

If you've ever had a physical injury that made walking difficult, you probably coped by favoring your injury—that is, by protecting the injured limb and eliminating nonessential activities.

We favor our injured parts by finding every conceivable way to reduce the number of painful movements we must make. Until the wound is healed, we park on the sidelines and live a "smaller" version of life.

The same is true when you have an emotional limp. On the subconscious level, your attention is focused on your injury. You favor your wound by reducing your life to survival mode. In an effort to avoid additional pain, you carefully monitor the environment for signs of danger, and you restrict your movements accordingly.

As long as the pain, which is rooted in the past, continues to dominate your present, you will be unable to live in the moment. As a result of this chronic inattention to real-time events, life will move on without you. In the end, you will be left with little more than a collection of painful memories and broken dreams.

GETTING PERSONAL

My childhood was painful. I believed that others saw me as being too much—too strong, too much of a dreamer, a person with too many big ideas, a person too big for my britches. Their words and actions told me: "Terri, you are less of a person than you think."

Their message came through loud and clear. The corollary also became obvious: because I received few expressions of love, I learned that, while I was *too big for my britches,* I was, at the same time, *not enough.*

From these signals, I extrapolated the belief that I was not worthy of love. That was the beginning of my limp. I assumed that if my parents, whom I considered to be all-knowing, found me unworthy of love, I must be inherently defective and uniquely unlovable.

This belief became the foundation of an even more serious, longer-term problem: the certainty that if those closest to me couldn't love me, surely no one could.

With this filter set firmly in place, the notion that I could be in any way loved by anyone was screened out of my perception. Since I was unworthy of love, then there must be a standard of love and approval I was incapable of meeting. Therefore, I was worthy of only one thing—rejection!

Despite my seeming unworthiness to be loved and the deficit of love and approval I experienced as a child, I continued my search for love and acceptance. I was so desperate that I even sought love from those whose attention was harmful to me. This pursuit continued into my adult life and played out through a variety of destructive choices and behaviors.

I've already shared one of my earliest manifestations of hiding. In the hopes of gaining approval (but not understanding that someone else's limp was the problem), I obediently made myself "smaller." In the process, I exchanged healthy elements of my identity for self-deprecating, self-destructive tendencies and coping behaviors.

Although I was born with a capacity to lead and naturally tended toward strength, I eventually retreated from my true identity. I sought to avoid the turbulence caused by living as my authentic self. By learning to behave in ways that didn't make waves, I learned how to earn "good girl" points. Although this brought fleeting moments of happiness, the real Terri had retreated into hiding, where she remained for decades.

Allow yourself to think about this, and be completely honest with yourself: Do you have a story that is in some way—in any way—similar to mine?

The fact is, everyone, whether they are able to admit it or not, has a story. *Every* family is dysfunctional in one way or another, and *every* living soul has been knocked about and bruised by life. Fortunately, *no one* has to stay in that condition. If you're willing to check your gait and *do something* to lose your limp, you *can* walk away from this chapter without your hobble.

Are you ready to take the plunge?

CREATE THE BOUNCE

As you may remember from Chapter 1, to create the bounce, you must first identify any misguided beliefs to which you may be clinging. Then you can replace them with new ways of thinking that move you toward your desired outcomes.

This exercise can help you take stock of where you are, not in terms of your behavior but in terms of your foundational attitudes and what they may be costing you.

Remember, while some attitudes may be obvious, the most pernicious ones can be hidden in emotional blind spots or covered over by performance fixes that mask your underlying fears.

You can uncover hidden attitudes by first identifying the recurring behaviors they produce. To gain insight, consider the following questions:

1. Do certain situations cause you to react in habitual ways? (For example, do you tend to get defensive when someone disagrees with you?)

2. Are you getting the results you desire, or are your reactions counterproductive? (For example, do emotional outbursts draw the attention you crave, or are you driving people further away?)

These self-defeating behaviors may be more readily evident to others than they are to you. Take time to reflect. Be painfully honest with yourself, but bear in mind that beating up on yourself is *not* the goal. The point is to take ownership of a misguided belief system and then make positive course adjustments so you can move forward.

There is no shame, only gain, in admitting negative attitudes. Shame tempts you to keep issues hidden, but bringing them to light will end the need for exhausting cover-ups.

So, go for it! Take charge of this moment by using every available avenue to root out the attitudes that have held you back. Speak them out, write them out...sing them out if you have to!

Below you'll find an expanded example and a few categories to help you get started. Grab a pen and paper and add categories as they apply to your life.

Example

Category: My appearance

What I Believe: I am not very pretty. Because I am tall and lanky, I stick out in a crowd, and I hate it!

What It Is Costing Me: I play down my appearance and avoid stylish clothing, hoping to blend in by being bland and inconspicuous. I don't bother with make-up or updating my hairstyle; it's not worth the effort. If I'm honest, not working with my appearance causes me to stand out even more and creates a new set of problems, including missed promotions at work, compromised relationships, and even physical symptoms resulting from my continual apprehensions about my appearance. Worst of all, I've lost opportunities to recognize my unique beauty and to develop the *me* inside.

The Bounce: Not everyone is a cover girl, and I don't have to be. I can take ownership and value myself by updating my wardrobe, making the best of my features, and having some fun with my hair! I can feel good about the attention of others, and I can smile knowing that I am qualified to reach for the stars.

Other Categories to Consider:

My personality

My intellect/education

My abilities/talents

My future

My relationships/marriage

How I believe others see me

Pay close attention to your feelings as you consider the different areas of your life. Allow yourself time to process your emotions. Writing is an amazing tool; write out your beliefs and the feelings attached to them. Then ask yourself this powerful question: *Where else is this belief showing up in my life, and what else is it costing me?*

Remember, take all the time you need for this important time of discovery; don't hurry! Your future is worth the investment. Rome wasn't built in a day, but it was *started* one day, and the day also came when it was completed!

SHAME IS THE FOUNDATION

Are you familiar with the story of Adam and Eve in the Garden of Eden? They were naked, yet without a care in the world. They weren't preoccupied with their state of undress; in fact, they didn't see themselves as being *un*dressed. They were clothed in the only fashion they'd ever known. They never questioned it or themselves. They were completely comfortable and wonderfully *un*self-conscious in their own skin.

That is, until the fateful day when, according to the biblical account, they sinned and their eyes were opened to the knowledge of good and evil. Suddenly, Adam and Eve were ashamed, and with shame came self-consciousness. Being naked was no longer acceptable, so they hid behind fig leaves. (See Genesis chapter 3.)

Many millennia later, shame is still the element that underlies our fears of rejection, abandonment, and failure. Shame is the sense that there is something "not right" about *who you are*. This is different from guilt, which relates to *what you have done*. Shame attaches itself directly to your identity and causes you to live in dread of the day when others will discover just how "not right" you really are.

Shame and the self-defeating behaviors it fosters can eclipse our most outstanding gifts and talents and suppress our vitality for life. Regardless of how shame enters our lives, it drives us, like Adam and Eve, into hiding at some level.

Whether you were:

- Ridiculed as a child for bedwetting

- Teased because you weren't as pretty or smart as someone

- Resented because your conception was unplanned

- Deserted by a parent or other important figure

- Laughed at, ridiculed, or ignored for any reason

...you have likely developed a belief system based in shame.

Shame will cause you to see yourself as *less than* others, different in some fundamental way and therefore deserving of less love, less happiness, less money, less success—less of everything. Because of shame, we develop the *expectation* that others will reject us. In fact, shame will cause us to believe that others *should* reject us. Then, without even realizing it, we train and provoke them to cast us aside.

Because our belief system governs our attitudes, supports our actions, and affects our gait, beliefs rooted in shame will cause us to behave in ways that make our most dreaded fears become self-fulfilling prophecies. Yet, when our worst nightmares become reality, we scratch our heads and wonder how in the world it came to be. Childhood dreams of accomplishing something meaningful will drift away until they are utterly out of reach. Sadly, we will believe that we are getting precisely what we deserve.

CHECKING THE GATE

Each time I complete a Hollywood stunt for film or television, the film crew pauses to do something called "checking the gate." That means they verify that the shot was actually captured on film and that it is good enough to be used. If the take is good, we can move to the next shot; if not, we must film it again.

From time to time in this book, we will pause to check the gate by considering the material and making sure we have successfully captured the meaning before we move on.

IT'S TIME TO LOSE THE MEASURING STICK

Every time you feel *less than* or *different from* others, you are judging yourself in comparison to an impossible standard of measurement. This invalid standard will cause your assessment to be misleading and will short-circuit the outcomes you long to experience.

For starters, comparing yourself to your notion of what other people are like is unrealistic. No two people on earth are alike. Applying such a standard creates a false comparison. It divides the world into two groups: you and the rest of the planet's six billion people.

When you try to be like everyone else...or *anyone* else...your self-assessment will be inaccurate, and you will miss this critical point: *Your strengths are not found in "same-ness," but in your uniqueness!*

Go ahead, lose the measuring stick! Refuse to confine yourself to a Barbie-doll mold. Give yourself permission to be one of a kind. Whatever your personality, appearance, or station in life, there is a "big" person living inside you...it is the *real you* who deserves to become all you were intended to be.

In the final analysis, you serve no one playing "small."

CHECK THE GATE

We've covered some very important territory in this chapter. Chances are, something that's been said has rung a bell for you. You might want to get a piece of paper, find a blank page in the book, or get a journal and write your answers to the following. These questions can help you assess and apply what you have discovered and get an understanding of where this self-discovery can take you:

1. What does your gait—your emotional posture—say to others? How does it make you feel and behave?

    _____

    _____

    _____

    _____

    _____

    _____

2. In what ways are you hiding? What does it give you (status quo, a sense of security, familiarity)? What is it costing you to hide (freedom, relationship, advancement)?

    _____

    _____

    _____

    _____

    _____

    _____

3. When do you notice that you feel shame? Can you trace the root of your shame to an incident or series of incidents in your life?

_____

_____

_____

_____

_____

_____

_____

_____

_____

_____

_____

_____

_____

_____

4. What faulty measuring stick have you been using on yourself?
   How has it skewed your sense of uniqueness and self-worth?

_____

_____

_____

_____

_____

_____

_____

_____

_____

_____

Don't be in a hurry to move on from the vein of thought this chapter has opened for you. You may want to re-read all or part of it. Whatever you do, don't go on without doing your homework by adhering to the following: checking your "gait," examining the ways in which you may be hiding, dealing with the shame issue, and tossing out the faulty measuring stick—once and for all.

Chapter 3

CAUGHT ON TAPE

S O many memorable days of stunt work have been etched in my mind, some of them probably forever. As you might imagine, many of my memories are thrilling. However, one film experience summons mixed emotions. This particular experience parallels my passage from the painful period of affirmation-seeking to the joyful era of my life "in the zone." The latter lifestyle is far superior; it allows me to be present in my professional moments of skilled and creative adventure rather than bogged down by the unmet (and often unmeet-able) need for love and approval.

On this particular film, I doubled the lead actress. She and I looked so much alike that people on the set often mistook one of us for the other. In fact, the resemblance was so strong that the director asked me to complete an action *and* acting sequence for the lead actress.

This doesn't happen every day, and although the scene was to be shot from behind, it was an extraordinary opportunity for me. The scene required lots of movement and was technically challenging, but when the director yelled, "Cut!" those of us in the scene (an actor and me) received a standing ovation.

What an intense experience! I felt like a million bucks, even after being pushed down the stairs, rolled down a hill four times, thrown out a door and down some more stairs, and roughed up in a series of domestic brawls (all of which gave me a thorough bruising up one side and down the other).

That's where the mixed emotions kick in, along with this sobering truth: the applause and accolades I received from those on the set did more than absorb the sting of the physical beating I had just endured. The affirmation also lifted the weight of a lifetime's worth of emotional beatings and impaired self-image.

Affirming words carried much-needed nourishment to my soul and alleviated my chronically unmet needs. For one fleeting moment, I felt validated and released from the stigma of being "less than enough." I came out from under the burden of shame that had held its grip on my self-esteem for so many years.

However, the positive effects of this affirmation would not be long-lasting, because my fundamental neediness was still driving my emotions. The praise I received was inebriating for the worst of all reasons: I was basing my self-worth on the signals sent by others. Emotionally speaking, I was the same ragdoll waiting to be acknowledged and scrambling for a morsel of affection to ease the ache in my heart.

My misery was so real back in those days that the mere memory of it causes my knees to buckle. How grateful I am for healing I have experienced—and how exciting it is to serve as an example of the healing that is available to other strong people who are hiding!

LIGHTS, CAMERA, ACTION!

Most likely, you don't remember this, but on the day you were born, some-one—a parent, a guardian, a nurse, *someone*—looked at you in amazement.

They heard your first cry, counted your tiny fingers and toes, and stood awestruck at the miracle of life. You were a sight to behold, and one look at you was enough to soften the hardest of hearts.

On that day, you knew no shame. You weren't trying to *do* anything, be anything, or prove anything—you simply *were*. Oblivious to the newborn in the next crib, you didn't care who was prettier or smarter. As far as ideas about self were concerned, you were a clean slate, perfectly content to be *you*.

Because you were born with an insatiable curiosity about your world and your place in it, you immediately began to take cues from others—from their touch, their tone of voice, and their words. You studied them and learned to respond in ways that seemed appropriate and met your needs. You smiled, you reached, you looked quizzically, and you even giggled. You paid careful attention, and in time, you began to grasp the meanings of words.

Before long, you were communicating with those around you through the use of language. With speech at your disposal and thoughts that could be expressed through speech, you formed memories that could be accessed later. Your mind became a storehouse of images. These images remained connected to the words and emotions that were part of your life story and therefore, your worldview.

Not every detail of every life experience is affixed to this mental footage. Countless mundane recollections wind up on life's cutting room floor. Yet, the images we consider to be the most significant remain etched in our memories, many of them forever.

Some people can remember experiences dating back to their days as toddlers; others cannot. What is your earliest childhood memory? You might recall opening presents under a Christmas tree or being zipped into a well-padded snowsuit. Maybe the sting of an immunization and the comforting response of a loving adult come to mind.

So many childhood memories are about things that *happened*, but the mind of a child also records more subtle messages, such as smiles received, murmurs whispered, hugs given, and hugs withheld. These identity-forming signals, whether positive or negative, are stored in memory, where they inform our beliefs and future behavior.

MISBELIEFS

These unchallenged erroneous notions about one's identity, worldview, and relationships with others are the foundation of unhealthy self-talk. Beliefs drive behavior; therefore, any misbeliefs that underpin the internal monologue will produce crippling emotions *and* inappropriate and self-destructive behaviors. Often, misbeliefs operate at the unconscious level (where unmet needs motivate us) so that we are completely unaware of their intrusion into the conduct of our lives.

SELF-TALK

This is the internal monologue, the mental footage comprised of words and images that play over and over in the mind from an early age. This monologue governs feelings, actions, beliefs, and habits and is the platform from which we interpret events, circumstances, and emotions. Harmful self-talk typically reflects the formation of misbeliefs; these distortions skew perception and force negative outcomes. Becoming aware of your self-talk is the first step to discovering what you believe at the most fundamental level.

What were the signals with which you grew up? Were you lavished with affirming words that gave you comfort and a sense of belonging? Did the actions of a parent or guardian demonstrate the desire to protect you from harm? Or were you spoken to harshly, made to feel like a nuisance, or even ignored?

For better or worse, the signals you received in those early days helped you to form the "measuring stick" you use to assess your status, especially in relation to others. These signals also helped you to answer the subliminal questions every child considers but rarely verbalizes:

Am I accepted?
Rejected?
Valued?
Wanted?

The signals you interpreted as answers to your unspoken questions formed your point of view. This perspective then became the basis of your beliefs about *self*. As long as the signals you received remain embedded and unchallenged in your memory, they continue to inform your sense of self-worth and your view of the world around you.

Think of it this way: once words and images are fixed in the file footage of your life story, they form a mental tape loop that plays over and over, forming your beliefs. These memories continually influence your thoughts, decisions, and expectations...of yourself, of others, of relationships, and of life's outcomes.

For some, the tape is affirming. It tells a positive story and aids in the development of a social and emotional groundedness or sense of security deep within one's heart. These positive signals speak to you throughout life's journey, reinforcing a healthy sense of self and delivering motivating messages that help you to move in the direction of your desired outcomes.

This inner security is reflected in several ways:

- In relationships, you are able to trust others because the tape tells you that the significant people in your life can be relied upon to love you.

- At work, you are confident of success because the tape says you are smart and capable.

- In the midst of a crisis, you have hope because the tape indicates that you are supported and capable of withstanding adversity.

Unfortunately, for many of us, the footage tells a less affirming story. Instead of creating a sense of acceptance, the images, voices, and emotions on the tape predict pending rejection and certain abandonment.

These dominating voices highlight every imperfection and magnify every failure, including those that have not yet occurred. The mental footage—in this case, the negative *self-talk* that plays in your head—reinforces the shame that underlies your fears. (Remember that shame insists that you are fundamentally defective and therefore unable to measure up to others.) Your self-talk intermingles with and reinforces your sense of shame, much the way carbon steel rebar strengthens concrete from within.

As long as the misbeliefs fixed in your memory go unchallenged, your life will play out in a reactive, defensive mode—a state of suspended animation that postpones authentic living and restricts your life to a hiding place where pain and loss can be avoided.

However, this avoidance comes at a very high cost. Consider some of the effects of negative self-talk:

- *It robs you of intimacy in relationships.* You must cover up emotionally, afraid to have your weaknesses exposed for fear you will be rejected.

- *It robs you of confidence at work.* You feel hopelessly inadequate compared to others. As a result, you fail to put forth your best effort. Instead, you live in fear of the day when the other shoe will drop and your inadequacies will be revealed.

- *It robs you of the ability to prevail during difficult times.* You are more easily overwhelmed by adverse circumstances because you feel unsupported, unloved, and unqualified to triumph.

The good news? You can integrate truthful beliefs into your self-talk and turn your internal monologue into a self-affirming stream that will sustain and continually refresh a joyful life!

STOP…REWIND…RE-RECORD

In Chapter 1, I shared with you the contents of the toxic script that ran through my head for decades. Like most people, I had long been unaware of the footage, or self-talk, that was playing on the big screen of my subconscious. You, too, may be dealing with some variation of this negative chatter, and you might not even know it.

You can be sure that, as long as the tape is running, you are *absorbing* the negative suggestions embedded within it. Unless you become consciously aware of the poisonous "music" playing in your head and do something to change it, negativity will continue to override truth in your life, creating the blind spots we discussed earlier. These filters will continue to screen out from your perception and your reality the very things you desire most. Among these filtered-out benefits are acceptance, contentment, peace, healthy relationships, and dreams of success.

I can hear you asking, "Whoa—are you saying I'm doomed to a life of failure and disappointment because noxious ideas have been running around my mind for so long?"

Absolutely not!

Out of the six-billion-plus people in the world, only you have the legitimate right to choose for yourself a better life. You do this, first of all, by carefully choosing what you will believe. You were created to be the director of your mind. You are *"at choice."* That is, you are empowered to decide what you will believe and how you will live in support of your beliefs.

As a child, you were powerless to select which content would be imprinted on your mental footage. Now, as an adult, you are in the driver's seat. You have sole authority over the content and duration of your thoughts. *At any time, you can stop the tape, rewind, and re-record.*

Stopping the tape. To regain control of your thought life and uproot self-degrading, self-defeating, and self-limiting thoughts, you must first become consciously aware of the footage that is running in your head. Then, instead of continuing as a passive recipient of mental content, you are invited to become an active participant in your thought-selection process.

When you identify self-sabotaging thoughts, simply stop the tape. Think of it as making an arrest. To *arrest* means to "seize" or "check the course of."[1] When the police become aware of a criminal on the loose, they don't wait for the offender to turn himself in. Instead, the police go on the offense. They focus their attention, energy, and resources on the task at hand: apprehending the suspect. They find out what he looks like, how he thinks, and where he hangs out. Then they do everything they can to flush him out of hiding and bring him to justice.

You can do the same with harmful self-talk. Become familiar with your thought life; learn to recognize the self-deprecating, self-limiting, and self-destructive thoughts that cross your mind. Then arrest those thoughts *every time they replay.* Incarcerate damaging ideas by denying them the freedom to assault your identity as a precious, gifted, and valuable human being.

Remember your world is framed by your thought life and the feelings that your thoughts promote. Therefore, the importance of stopping the tape cannot be overstated. Your worldview *will* determine your behavior and your life outcomes. When you arrest your negative self-talk, you place yourself in a position to change the direction of your life.

Rewinding the tape. Once you have arrested negative self-talk, continue investigating your thought life. Rewind the tape and examine its contents more closely. It is important to separate truth from distortion (what I call "the stories we tell ourselves"). Then determine how much credence you want to give to the thoughts that have governed your life to this point. Evaluate the various sources of your negative self-talk. For example, you'll probably find that the negative lessons others "taught" you about yourself sprang not from a defect within you but from a hurt that was driving them at an unconscious level.

While you're investigating, search for evidence of misbeliefs that may be contradicting your professed desires. Do you long to be married, yet find yourself withdrawing from relationships when they become serious? Patterns like this can demonstrate the operation of a misbelief. In this case, the outward profession is. *I want to be married.* However the misbelief overrides the conscious desire, saying, *Marriage is scary—it would expose me to further rejection or abandonment. I can't take that risk again.*

Face counterproductive thoughts head-on. If you discover a fear of commitment, admit it and own it. Then choose what action you will take concerning your fear. If someone has rejected you, arrest your thoughts and rewind the tape by asking yourself these questions:

- Do I reject myself?

- How does their rejection relate to me? Is it even about me?

- What positive outcome can I take away from this encounter?

Make every negative that rears its ugly head an opportunity to renegotiate, not what has already happened, but where you will go from here. By rewinding the tape, you position yourself to be at choice. You are not stuck with whatever is on your mental footage. Instead, you are serving notice of your decision to change the course of your life. In essence, you are saying:

I defiantly refuse to be subject to the mess that went on in years past. I have suffered loss because of my choices and the choices made by others, but no more. What happened cannot be undone; however, I refuse to allow the effects of the past to control me. I am no longer a victim; I choose the attitude (the emotional backbone) of a victor.

Re-recording the tape. "OK," you say, "I hear the words of my inner monologue, and I am learning to differentiate between healthy and unhealthy thoughts. But I feel hopelessly mired in old information. How can I possibly dig out?"

Hopelessness can only survive in the absence of perceived alternatives. If you're like most people, you've never considered the possibility that your thought life (including that which functions at the subconscious and unconscious levels) can be directed by the conscious decisions you are at choice to make.

More often than not, this truth comes as a revelation when suddenly we realize that the thoughts already in our minds are not the only ones from which we can choose.

Arresting your internal monologue and rewinding the tape will interrupt your thoughts and provide an opportunity to regroup. But the next step—perhaps the most important step of all—is to actually reframe your thinking by replacing the negative elements of your mindset with new, life-giving ideas.

When you reframe your thought life, you rewire the patterns by which your brain processes information, and you afford yourself the opportunity to dig out from the ways of the past. Regardless of how long a counterproductive belief system has impacted the course of your life or how strong or weak you perceive yourself to be, you *can* change your thinking. Consider it a mental tune-up: first, you scrape away the old, rusty thinking that you thought was your only alternative:

- I am destined to fail just as my father said I would.

- No one loves me because there is nothing good about me.

- Others deserve the things I desire; therefore, they are able to prosper and I am not.

Then you add new spark plugs to your belief system by embracing the positive ideas that can empower you to reach your desired outcomes. Consider replacing the rust with the following spark-plug beliefs:

- Nobody but me can decide whether I will succeed or fail.

- I am a marvelous creation worthy of the acceptance of others.

- My inherent value is found in my humanity; therefore, I am as deserving of prosperity as anyone else is.

A change in your thinking, and therefore in your life, is always an available option! Regardless of what happened yesterday, you are in the driver's seat of your life today. When it looks as though your life has spun completely out of your control, take a closer look; the steering wheel is still firmly in your grasp.

The problem is never how to get new, innovative thoughts into your mind, but how to get old ones out. Every mind is a building filled with archaic furniture. Clean out a corner of your mind and creativity will instantly fill it.[2]

—Dee Hock
Founder and former CEO of VISA

MORE THAN THE POWER OF POSITIVE THINKING

Reframing your thought life is not about plucking happy little thoughts out of thin air. It is about aligning your thoughts with objective truth so that you can live as your authentic self and move in the direction of your destiny.

A word of caution about truth: it is a sword that cuts both ways. It sparks freedom, sometimes in an instant, but it often does so by uncovering issues we'd just as soon leave hidden. As we've already discovered, a search for truth can subject us to rude awakenings of one sort or another, times when the truth we crave makes us painfully aware of a character flaw, bad decision, or unhealthy pattern.

Emotions are meant to be felt, not suppressed or ignored. Pain is a powerful alert system that calls our attention to something that needs fixing. Therefore, painful discoveries of truth are opportunities to find wholeness. If we pay attention to the alert system, we position ourselves to address our needs and move forward. We make way for emotions to be processed and to pass safely through us without creating new wounds and expending unnecessary energy.

Suppose you feel abandoned by your mate and discover that you have actually driven your partner away with incessant demands and overbearing neediness. As painful as this realization would be, it is also an opportunity to correct the course of the relationship and achieve future success.

Maybe you have suffered the loss of a job, never realizing that your tendency to criticize others has undermined your value to the firm—even though you were the most skilled member of the team. As humbled as you might be by the experience, imagine how much better prepared you are to succeed in your next position.

Every confrontation with truth can bring us closer to our desired outcomes, but only if we will own the truth and embrace the pain it brings as being part of the growth process. Nothing good or lasting comes without effort. As the saying goes, *No pain, no gain.*

CREATE THE BOUNCE

Invest some quality time to monitor the voices that have helped to form distortions of your self-image. Do this by first stopping the tape, then rewinding it to investigate the content. Identify any negative themes playing in your head; arrest these destructive thoughts and confront them head on.

If you find it difficult to discern your negative self-talk (as I did at first), begin with what I call a "noticing period," during which you simply take notice of the images, thoughts, and words crossing your mind.

Create an atmosphere of stillness and set aside the time to listen. Jot down any words and phrases that come up. You may be surprised at what is being said on the inside and amazed at the things you had not noticed before!

Another way to identify negative themes is to look for areas in your life that are inconsistent with your desired outcomes. Ask yourself whether misbeliefs could be producing any unfavorable results that you may be experiencing.

Consider the sources of these misbeliefs and evaluate the validity of those sources. Ask yourself whether what you believe is truth or a story you are telling yourself (or allowing someone else to convince you of). Then consider how such stories may have sabotaged the outcomes you have experienced so far.

Finally, begin the process of re-recording your mental footage. Reframe your thinking by replacing the negative elements in your belief system with statements based in truth.

One way to begin this process of reframing your thoughts is to consider the negative nicknames parents and others may have given you as a child. There's an old nursery rhyme that says, "Sticks and stones may break my bones, but names will never hurt me." Nothing could be further from the truth. Names are words, and words have the power to build up or tear down, create or destroy. Misbeliefs often develop from the words people speak to us, particularly during childhood.

For example, you may have been named: *lazy, stupid, ridiculous, helpless, too tall, too short, too slow, too fast, too fat, too lanky*. You may have been told that children should be "seen and not heard," and you may have translated it to mean, "*You don't have anything worthwhile to say, so just shut up.*"

Use the space provided below to jot down the lies you have come to believe. Then take ownership of your misbeliefs by writing down new, truthful expressions that are aligned with your hopes and dreams. (See the example provided.)

Whenever the old, self-defeating tapes replay in your head, arrest them and reframe your thoughts to line up with more helpful, truthful ideas. Do this faithfully, over and over again. You will see your attitude change, and it will cause your circumstances to change as well!

Old Recurring Thoughts

Example: Nothing will ever go my way because smarter, quicker people will always beat me to the punch.

New Replacement Thoughts

Example: My life is filled with opportunities to excel, and I am up to the task.

Your story is yours, and only yours, to write. The trappings of victory won't appear the instant you change course; you must allow time and patience for the process and trust in its power to transform. Fully embrace the challenge of developing new ways of thinking. Your destination will begin to change the moment you do.

Go ahead—reframe your thinking and rewrite the outcomes of the coming chapters in your life story!

You are a person *at choice*!

Chapter 4

SHATTER YOUR
INVISIBLE WHEELCHAIR

PERHAPS you've heard the axiom, *"Fact is stranger than fiction."* Although it may seem cliché, true stories are often more bizarre than anything concocted by Hollywood writers. Even for those of us who work in the film industry and see unimaginable things brought to life on a daily basis, the old saying holds true.

Every working day, whether in the studio or on location, I am prepared to be flung around in some new and usually insane way. Later, when I see the stunt onscreen or as we check the gate (verify the footage) immediately after filming, I am amazed at the sight of my ragdoll-like body being thrown about. The funny thing to me—or perhaps *ridiculous* is a more appropriate word—is that, although I am a sane person, I actually *enjoy* doing this risky type of work.

Having read this far, you are already aware that the chaos in my life wasn't always chaos of the controlled variety. Before I broke out of my emotional hiding place, *ragdoll* was an apt word to describe my identity. I saw myself as a fragmented, torn-apart soul, and I fully expected to be tossed around by fate. I had internalized the misbelief that my life was in the hands of others and completely out of my control. It had not even occurred to me that other choices were possible! My assumed role was that of a bystander whose assignment was to take the hits for everybody else. Unlike my experiences as a stuntperson, I took those hits with no upside—no pay, no input, no glory.

There seemed to be no room for me to *live* as a full-fledged, whole, valuable individual who could spread her wings and occupy a unique place in the world. So, I learned to *exist*, virtually imprisoned, wherever I happened to land. More often than not, I could be found crushed at the feet of someone to whom I had given away my personal power—that is, my right as a human being to determine both the quality and direction of my life.

Finally, many years before I began working as a stuntperson, the day came when I, the unwitting ragdoll, hit the ground once again—*literally*. It was not a stunt, and there was no safety net; this was my real life, a life devoid of mercy.

This day was not so unusual; I had absorbed many such hits over the years, but this time I responded in a new way. The change was barely perceptible at the time, but it was enough to begin a cycle of recovery and restoration.

This time, instead of passively observing the scene of my personal tragedy and burying it in numbed, unexpressed emotions, I took stock of the ravaged state to which I had driven myself. As dismal a scene as it was, it is where my breakthrough began.

My injuries on that pivotal day were emotional *and* physical. After a night of partying at a local club, my boyfriend was driving me home. Although I was still plagued by internal fears, the appearance I projected was one of *fearlessness*. After years of hiding and blaming others, my fear had become a shield of polished anger designed to protect my injured soul. The aggressive personality and sharp tongue on the outside masked the hurt and pain inside.

Riding in the passenger seat that night, I was incensed over a remark my boyfriend had made, and I grabbed the stereo remote to change the music that was playing. From behind the steering wheel, my boyfriend lunged for the remote. Defiant, I held it out of his reach. In a rage, he grabbed me by the hair, thrust my skull into the windshield, and simultaneously slammed the brakes, increasing the force with which my head struck the windshield. I remember being amazed at how much damage my head caused to the car.

The next thing I knew, my boyfriend flung open the passenger door, yanked me from the car, and threw me onto the street. He sped off as I lay heaped in a bloody, crumpled mess on the pavement. With the side of my face pressed against the greasy gutter, I heard the sound of water gurgling as waste flowed through the sewer below. It was a moment of startling clarity in which I recognized the sickening place I was in and the unacceptable self-image I had embraced. I knew that if I wanted to survive, physically or emotionally, I had to realize I was *at choice,* and I had to take action *immediately*.

As I pushed myself up from the pavement, I cried out to Heaven for the grace and mercy I needed to move toward healing and out of the stark jungle my life had become. At that moment, I experienced what can only be called a revelation: I recognized, for the first time, that *it was within my power to decide where I would go from there.*

No one with a megaphone had hiked through the underbrush to save me as happened in the story of Lieutenant Onoda. Instead, I had re-connected with myself, the authentic Terri I had abandoned so many years earlier. By simply owning my woundedness, I had found the rescuer within and gingerly made my way out of my self-imposed prison.

As I walked the familiar route toward home, I knew I was headed in a new direction. Even though all of the shattered pieces of my life did not come together instantly on that dark street corner, I knew my life would never be the same. I had made a noteworthy choice to live in the present tense, to regain control of my life, and to accept the risks my new choices would bring.

IDENTIFY EMOTIONAL PARALYSIS

If you have ever experienced a tidal wave of fear, you probably know what it is to stand outside yourself, frozen in a state of passivity and hopelessness. You may be experiencing this kind of paralysis right now as a reaction to any number of challenges threatening to overwhelm you. These mesmerizing ordeals come in many forms, including, but not limited to:

- Financial devastation

- Catastrophic illness

- Physical abuse

- Divorce

- Death of a loved one

- Loss of a job

Emotional paralysis is not unusual. Quite the contrary, this type of suspended animation is a common default reaction to situations and circumstances we perceive to be beyond our ability to control. In those defining moments when we assess ourselves to be helpless, we become as the proverbial deer caught in the headlights; we stand frozen, quite literally paralyzed in the darkness. The car is speeding toward us, but we do nothing to save ourselves.

If we allow ourselves to drift deeper into the netherworld of perceived powerlessness, this passive reaction becomes an almost involuntary reflex, much like a physical knee-jerk reaction. Instead of being moved to action by a worsening situation, we become increasingly inclined to accept the status quo and watch things happen—*to* us and *around* us. We become accustomed to behaving as though we have no say in the matter, as though we have no power, as though we don't even have the right to desire or to initiate change.

This phenomenon is what I call life in an *invisible wheelchair*. That is a strong term, but an accurate one. Although this wheelchair exists only in the realm of the mind and emotions, it is as rigid and restrictive as one made of steel. The perceived powerlessness it promotes is not helpful, but disabling—emotionally, socially, and over time, even physically.

Who is immune to this experience? No one. Every human being experiences a sense of helplessness at some level or on some occasion, because every person on the planet has faced circumstances that seem bigger than his or her ability to overcome.

Truth be told, there *are* situations that are beyond our control. Consider those who were slaughtered when 767s flew through their office windows on September 11, 2001. Their fear was not misplaced, nor was their helplessness imagined.

However, we often feel inadequate to rise above the most ordinary situations, simply because misplaced fear speaks to us with such authority. This fear is not healthy but counterproductive; it's the enemy of our souls. It is the fear that screams from the internal tapes we talked about in the Chapter 3. It tells us what we *can't accomplish*, what we'll *never have*, and where we *cannot go*.

Fear is an invisible enemy that roars loud enough to commandeer our attention. Although you can't see fear, its effects are easy to spot. You can compare its action to that of the wind. If you have ever experienced a hurricane, you've seen not the wind itself but the effects of the wind: debris flying everywhere, rooftops being lifted off their moorings, and reporters standing sideways against the onslaught of its fierce currents.

When the wind of fear is blowing, its effects are equally apparent. In "fight or flight" situations, for example, your heart begins to race, your palms sweat, your stomach churns, and you desperately seek a way of escape.

Non-life-threatening circumstances can also cause you to fear. Conflicts with co-workers, the loss of a job, or trouble in a relationship can elicit a broad range of fear-related responses, including sleeplessness and appetite loss, lack of concentration, and depression, to name but a few.

Fear can also raise your level of self-doubt, reinforce your distrust of others, and prompt you to withdraw inside yourself until the perceived danger blows over. Ironically, this tendency to isolate ourselves is heightened precisely when input from others could be most helpful.

Although you can detect the effects of fear in your emotions, you might not recognize fear as the actual culprit. In our minds, fear-driven reactions become closely intertwined with the events that prompted them. In reality, the feelings associated with fear are triggered by our perception of those events. This distinction between events and the fear that follows is an important one if fear—particularly misplaced fear—is to be successfully uprooted.

Just as fear produces a wide variety of symptoms, it also is the source of a broad range of behaviors. For some people, fear produces timidity. Others display their struggle with fear through repeated outbursts of anger and an inordinate need to be confrontational or controlling. (Please note: The intensity of these behaviors is in direct correlation to the level of fear [*i.e.*, the greater the need to control, the higher the level of internal fear].)

Perhaps the most common reaction to fear is passivity, which is the choice to make no choice at all. When we talked about checking your gait, we touched on the nonverbal signals a passive posture transmits. When withdrawal and inaction become your habitual responses to fear, your low-key behavior can be misconstrued by others as disinterest, laziness, or lack of ambition.

However, withdrawal and inaction (or hiding) is often rooted more deeply, not in an individual's personality traits, but in what his or her "misbelief system" dictates. When fear reigns, it clutters the emotional environment and inhibits personal growth. Imagine trying to see through a window screen that is gummed up with dirt and other particles so that you can barely see through the mesh. Not only is your vision impaired by the accumulated grit and grime, but the dirty screen also keeps fresh air from coming inside.

When fear is in operation, your vision is obscured; you can't see outside yourself clearly, and light is not allowed in. Fear distorts reality; it magnifies adversity so that every challenge is perceived as an insurmountable obstacle, rather than an opportunity to transcend the circumstances and experience victory.

Fears based in shame, rejection, and abandonment can imprison you, figuratively speaking, by binding you into an invisible wheelchair. However, this debilitation is only possible when you permit your fears to operate undercover. How can this covert operation gain the upper hand? Simply by your choice not to confront fear. This choice to shrink from the challenge is a classic example of how to give away your personal power.

The way to defuse fear is to become proactive—uncover the fear, own it, and expose it to the light of day. Quit playing the blame game. Pointing fingers is the opposite of owning your fear, and unless you own it, you're stuck living with its detriments. However, when you face your fears, they lose their power over you, because their deception is exposed. Exposing your fears empowers you to confront them rationally, rather than reflexively, and will enable you to *detect* the invisible wheelchair to which you are confined.

When I first detected my invisible wheelchair, I realized I would have to kick my way out of it and shatter it once and for all. It required me to take notice and then action. That's where the breakthrough began!

That is my intention in writing this book—for you to experience the same freedom and for you to first *unmask,* then *shatter* your emotional wheelchair and leap to freedom.

GETTING PERSONAL

My invisible wheelchair has been shattered, yet I remember it clearly. It was incredibly sturdy even though it was constructed of nothing but pure, unadulterated fear.

The fear to which I succumbed was powered by my perception of what others expected of me. I accepted what they said and tacitly agreed to their demands. Can you see how much power I gave away? Can you see how I placed my personal power on a silver platter and handed it to others?

Whether these expectations were real or imagined really didn't matter; either way, they produced a palpable effect. Some of the expectations by which I was bound came in the form of the instructions implied by others. For example, I grew up with the perception that I was to speak only when spoken to and do only what I was directed to do.

These expectations by the significant people in my life became my sole guideline for living. As a dutiful child who trusted my adult loved ones implicitly (as most children do), I was obedient and compliant, always afraid to disappoint them.

Without realizing it, I had dismantled the parts of my authentic identity that seemed to be in conflict with the instructions I received. In the process, I allowed the place of my emotional confinement to be reinforced. In essence, I carried within myself an unwritten rule that stated, *I am at your mercy.* Out of that belief flowed my behavior: I placed myself completely at the mercy of the beliefs and desires of others.

In the third grade, I became consciously aware of my invisible wheelchair and cognizant of how deeply withdrawn I had become. I lived not in the world with everybody else but somewhere deep inside my own head. From my hiding place within, I could stifle my own voice and keep the low profile I thought would shield me from further emotional injury.

When hidden from others and insulated from the worrisome task of being me, I felt relatively safe. I was afraid to face the consequences that living in my authentic identity would bring; I found comfort in my invisible wheelchair.

The day would come when safety was no longer a sufficient incentive to remain in bondage. Freedom became the higher goal. At that point, the shattering of my invisible wheelchair would become imperative.

But that would take some time.

In the truest sense, freedom cannot be bestowed; it must be achieved.[1]

—Franklin D. Roosevelt
Speech, September 22, 1936

The Deception of the Slow Boil

You may be wondering how someone with a strong personality and big dreams could submit herself to the death-like existence I have described.

Perhaps it can be explained with two analogies. The first is the fable of the frog placed in a kettle of water and slowly boiled to death. The ill-fated frog offered no resistance to his terrible situation, because he failed to recognize where his trip to the pot was really headed.

The frog's first moments in the kettle seemed tolerable enough. The water temperature was mild, much like the creek in summertime. The unsuspecting frog frolicked just as he was accustomed to doing in his familiar habitat.

Meanwhile, the water temperature was slowly rising. But because the change was incremental, the frog's sinewy body adjusted, little by little. The unsuspecting creature was lulled into complacency and only too late would he realize the gravity of his situation. By then he was doomed, and death ensued.

The second analogy that applies is that of the slaves you read about in an earlier chapter. Even after a kind traveler had set them free, they chose to remain within several feet of their former prison. Over the course of their years of enslavement, they had gradually grown comfortable with their shackles so that even after their chains had been cut away, the men *chose* to live as captives restricted to familiar, non-threatening surroundings.

Similar scenarios play out daily in our modern world. In your city, on this very day, there are men or women who have returned to prison after a period of freedom in the outside world. Ostensibly, they are back in prison because they are suspected, or convicted, of having committed a crime.

Yet, for some returning inmates, the reason they have been re-incarcerated is far more nuanced. Once they have repaid their debt to society, many ex-convicts find life outside prison intimidating, even overwhelming.

Suddenly, the everyday choices they longed to be able to make are something to be feared. Old voices of insecurity and fear begin to play on the unhealed self-image. Deep down, the ex-con becomes convinced that the familiarity and simplicity of prison life are easier to deal with than the complexities of life outside the prison gate.

Freedom is not free, as the saying goes. It comes at a price. It requires, among other things, the making of choices every day. Freedom is an invitation to take ownership of your life and everything that affects your life. That means you must *choose* personal responsibility, change, growth, and the voluntary observance of society's rules.

In a brick-and-mortar prison, the inmate's freedom to choose is surrendered. Inmates don't get to vote or decide what to wear. They can't even decide when they will see their loved ones. They have no say in the matter. The responsibility for these decisions rests in the hands of the appropriate appointed authorities.

For most people, inmates included, the thought of such a complete loss of control is mortifying. Yet, for those who grow accustomed to it, prison can provide a counterfeit sense of safety and security, despite the inherent dangers associated with prison life.

The invisible wheelchair offers a similar, equally deceptive, sense of comfort. It offers an existence in which the occupant becomes unduly dependent upon others and therefore enslaved to them. In the invisible wheelchair, you surrender your right to be your authentic self, and you submit to inappropriate, misplaced authority.

Why would anyone do this to themselves? The answer is simple—many believe it to be their only choice. When emotional paralysis strikes, surrender can look like the only conceivable way to deal with the overwhelming fear of rejection and abandonment.

WHAT ARE YOU TOLERATING?

A hot-button word in today's world is *tolerance*, which, taken at face value, is a good thing. "Good" tolerance is the polar opposite of bigotry and tyranny: we respect those whose race, ethnicity, culture, religion, or opinion differs from our own.

Yet, when it comes to racism, ethnic cleansing, and unethical practices, tolerance is a travesty. These abuses are never acceptable; to tolerate them would be inappropriate and detrimental to those who are abused and to society at large.

Remember our pitiful frog? He became comfortable with a hazardous situation because he had learned, little by little, to tolerate an untenable environment. For a while, he was blissfully unaware of his impending doom, but at some point, complacency exacted its price!

Imagine for a moment a less dramatic example of behavior that should not be tolerated. Let's assume that a young lady is so infatuated with her boyfriend that she puts up with being stood up by him, week in and week out.

This tolerance raises a red flag. A confident young woman with a healthy self-image, good role models, and a strong support system would not abide this behavior for long. She would quickly realize that her inconsiderate beau isn't the only fish in the sea.

But a young woman who views herself with a "less than" mindset and believes herself to be unworthy of attention or consideration, undesirable or unattractive, or ineligible to be loved for the person she is might consider mistreatment as the price she must pay to be accepted *by someone*. In her case, the desperate unmet need for attention and approval could override self-respect and erode healthy boundaries. In an effort to get her needs met, this young girl might willingly exchange the dream of a sound, fulfilling relationship for a quick fix of self-esteem.

Much like the frog who endures the slow boil, she may not see the long-term consequences of her misplaced tolerance. As she trains herself to dutifully absorb the impact of her boyfriend's inappropriate tendencies, the young woman's emotional pain threshold will rise incrementally until she becomes desensitized to abuse. Because she fears being alone, she will submit to the demands of an unhealthy relationship.

Over the longer term, seemingly minor instances of misplaced tolerance can lead to the gradual acceptance of overtly abusive treatment. The insecure woman's invisible wheelchair can become more heavily reinforced and confining with each demeaning experience until the day comes when she is completely enslaved and shackled by emotional dependency.

WE TEACH OTHERS HOW TO TREAT US

How is such an unhealthy progression set in motion? In part, inappropriate treatment escalates because misplaced tolerance signals approval for bad behavior. In other words, inappropriate submission trains others to see the "tolerant" party the way they see themselves: as *"less than."*

It is important to be reminded of a critical point before we continue:

It is *never* appropriate to take advantage of or to abuse anyone, regardless of his or her behavior or projected self-image. No one deserves to be abused—*not ever!*

The fact remains: one party's (inappropriately) submissive tendencies can feed the other's (inappropriate) need for control. The young girl in our story has blind spots that predispose her to certain negative situations. Meanwhile, her boyfriend has issues of his own. If he had come to the relationship emotionally healthy, he would have responded to the woman's brokenness by facilitating healing and promoting healthier interaction.

An important part of becoming free from your invisible wheelchair is to ask yourself, *How am I training others to treat me, and what adjustments do I want to make?* Until you realize that...

- You have inherent worth and value...

- There is a unique purpose and plan for your life...

- You are loveable...

- You can be your authentic self without guilt or shame...

...you will not treat yourself with dignity, nor will you expect others to do so. As long as that is the case, you will be overlooked and dismissed by others, just as you overlook and dismiss yourself.

The relationship scenario I've described is merely an example, and an over-simplified one at that. For some it may not resonate, but for others it might inspire an "a-ha" moment. Whether you recognize yourself as someone who has trained others to act inappropriately, allowed the slow boil to become a way of life, or taken refuge in passivity—take heart. It's never too late to change your direction!

CHECK THE GATE

Self-discovery results from an encounter with truth. As you read this chapter, you may have readily identified with the discussion of emotional paralysis or life in the invisible wheelchair. But perhaps you're uncertain whether these issues connect with your life.

Use the following questions to help you "locate" yourself in relation to these issues. Allow any emotionally paralyzing patterns in your life to be exposed to your scrutiny. Embrace freedom by being transparent with yourself as you consider your responses to the following questions:

1. When was the last time you felt so intimidated in an everyday situation that you backed away from it entirely? Describe the circumstances.

2. What fear has caused you to avoid certain situations, people, personalities, or opportunities? Does the fear you have identified qualify as truth, or is it a story that you have embraced?

3. Where have you experienced, and inadvertently adjusted to, the "slow boil" in some area of your life? Is someone taking greater and greater advantage of you? What would your life look like if you showed a healthy intolerance in this case?

4. Think about interactions with those closest to you, particularly where you have experienced frustration, dissonance (lack of harmony), and or emotional suffering. Consider the following:

   a. What is being reflected to you in those interactions?

   b. How do you feel in those interactions? Describe your emotions.

   c. Where else might these effects be showing up in your life?

   d. Write down one action you will take to own where you are and to step out of the boiling pot.

   e. As you commit to making an internal adjustment, notice any shifts in emotion or experience that occur.

On each page of this book, you are discovering tools to turn the tide in your life and create a momentum of improving results. You have learned to check your gait and have become more aware of the messages you send yourself. You know how attitudes affect your emotional posture and how you are empowered to make adjustments.

You have also learned how to handle the negative messages others have conveyed over the years; you have learned how to stop the tape and re-record it with the encouraging, supportive voices of truth.

In this chapter, I've encouraged you to examine your heart for patterns that might be keeping you confined to an emotional wheelchair. In the next chapter, you will learn how to stand up and shatter that invisible wheelchair by digging out the root of shame.

Ready for a little gardening?

Chapter 5

UNMASK YOUR AUTHENTIC IDENTITY

O N a film set, scores of professionals, each of whom possesses a specific skill set, work in tandem to bring each cinematic shot to completion.

Although this well-oiled machine works flawlessly most of the time, the potential for unintended chaos is always present. If order breaks down on the set, catastrophes can happen, and when timelines and budgets go awry, stunts become increasingly dangerous and even deadly.

For a film shoot to be successful, there must be absolute clarity about each contributor's role. Directors, actors, stunt people, and all other crew members have specific assignments. The costume designer does not direct the film, and prop people don't make changes to the script. These clear distinctions as to professional identity are designed to prevent chaos and ensure a smooth operation.

Once the film is released and moviegoers flock to theatres to see it, a new dynamic takes over, one that blurs identity distinctions on purpose. For a movie to tell its story in a believable manner, it must be shot and edited with a pinch of deception. This enables viewers to enjoy the film experience by suspending their beliefs about what is real and what is staged.

Here's how it works: When you dig into your popcorn and watch a movie, you enter the realm of illusion. In this realm, identities are switched, not to foster confusion, but in order to trick the mind of the viewer into accepting the unfolding story as reality.

When you watch *Gone With the Wind*, the characters must be brought to life in such a way that you will be able to set aside your knowledge of Clark Gable, the actor, and see him as Rhett Butler, the man who loves Scarlett O'Hara.

When Clark Gable smiles, you must see Rhett Butler smiling. And when Vivien Leigh pouts, you must buy into the identity switch long enough and with sufficient abandon so that you believe that she *is* Scarlett O'Hara, a southern belle who can pout like no other.

Where stunts are concerned, the suspension of the real world and the creation of a believable new reality must go a step further. When Scarlett tumbles down the grand staircase, neither she nor Vivien Leigh is actually falling.

Enter the third identity: the stuntperson. Regardless of whether the stuntperson resembles Vivien Leigh, the illusion that she is Scarlett must be seamless. If the viewer is unconvinced, this pivotal, powerful scene would have been ineffective and even laughable.

MISTAKEN EMOTIONAL IDENTITY

This harmless game of mistaken identity works its magic countless times during a movie. Because it works so well, actors can act without risking life and limb, stunt people can blend art and science to create thrilling action scenes, and moviegoers can get their money's worth.

In real life, however, distorted, hidden, misrepresented, and inauthentic identities caused by shame have far more serious implications. These façades hide the emotional disfigurement and bruising shame causes. These masks confine their wearers to the invisible wheelchair and the state of emotional paralysis.

This was certainly true in my case. I believed my only worth as a person came from the value others were willing to ascribe to me. I placed my significance in their hands, hoping they would give me worth. It was an unfair transaction; I disadvantaged and placed myself at the mercy of others. I also left them to carry an impossible burden—responsibility for the health of my self-image.

If you could have seen inside my emotional prison cell, you would have sensed the deadness of the place. The heaviness of my shame weighed upon my countenance. You would have noticed my eyes darting to avoid meeting yours; you would have detected the quick crumbling of the smile I could not sustain.

Because I believed I was inferior by design, I was fully invested in a debased and mistaken identity. That is the essence of shame. The authentic me—the creative, resourceful, valuable person God created—was buried beneath layers of fear and self-doubt.

This debasement happened incrementally. Each time I compromised my inherent worth to gain approval, I gave away another piece of myself and strengthened the misbeliefs underpinning my shame.

Fear became my master. I allowed it to not only rule but also to enslave me. I was plagued by many profound fears, all triggered by the shame of what I *believed* to be my deficient identity. I feared being authentic because I *believed* that:

- I would fail to meet the expectations of others.

- My shortcomings and fears would be exposed.

- I would be rejected or abandoned because the authentic Terri was either "too much" or "not enough."

My fears were symbiotically connected; they fed off one another, breeding a downward spiral of shame and destruction by which I became further and further disconnected from my authentic self.

My downward spiral demonstrated the vicious cycle of shame:

1. My fears were set in motion by what I perceived to be disparaging signals sent by others.

2. My fears were nourished and reinforced by my unrelenting internal monologue.

3. My fears were fulfilled in disappointing outcomes because I made fear-based choices guaranteed to yield those outcomes.

4. The fulfillment of my fears further distorted my self-image; each outcome served as tangible proof that I was *less than*.

The dents in my self-image were caused in part by my thinking: I had a sense of my shortcomings and what *I should have been*. This was an unattainable identity conjured with the faulty measuring stick we talked about earlier.

This standard was arbitrary and always out of reach. I can remember having the recurring and overwhelming thought, *Even if I were president of the United States, I would not be good enough.* Even if I dreamed of soaring to unreachable heights, I was still the lowest of the low, living by the unwritten rule that said, *I am at your mercy.* Except for my earliest years, I was never really at the mercy of anyone but myself.

Freedom was what I outwardly desired, but I used the *familiarity* of my invisible wheelchair to hold freedom at bay. I continued to blame others for my emotional paralysis, so that I could subconsciously justify my hiding place. *I had not yet reached the point where I wanted healing more than I wanted those responsible to acknowledge and feel my pain.*

This not only kept the "inner me" in an invisible wheelchair, but it also stifled my outward life. This sense of confinement bred frustration and was a direct reflection of the self-limiting monologue playing inside my head. My faulty belief system had overwritten the truth about the person I was created to be; therefore, my life outcomes were confined to the limits *I* had established.

Because I had given away my power, my publicly displayed persona was controlled and self-limiting. What others saw was not authentically me. Instead, it was what I feared and distrusted most—it was a façade.

Unlike our *Gone With the Wind* example, this case of mistaken identity was not harmless. It was a pernicious and deeply injurious substitution by which I traded the sanctity of my authenticity for the distorted self-image of a powerless, hopeless, inanimate ragdoll, who happened to be hiding behind a strong outward image.

BACK TO THE BASICS ABOUT FEAR

By now you probably have a keen awareness of the destructive potential of fear. You may have identified specific fears that confine you to your invisible wheelchair. This is a strong beginning, but our ultimate goal is to *shatter your invisible wheelchair*. To do so, we must pull up the roots of shame and unravel the fabric of fear.

First, recognize that fear is a real emotion, even when it is sparked by something imagined. Fear arises in response to something perceived to be threatening. Fear can be triggered by:

- Events that seem beyond our control

- Outcomes that appear to be threatening

- Setbacks we've suffered

- Real, exaggerated, or imagined threats to our well-being.

We discover the roots of our fears by looking beneath the foundation to the bedrock on which fear rests, which is *shame*.

Let's consider an example: Imagine that a long-awaited opportunity (a better job, lucrative business venture, or marriage) has just come your way.

After the initial rush of excitement and adrenaline subsides, what emotions surface? Do you have misgivings? Are they based in a realistic assessment of shortcomings or warning signs (*i.e.*, the business requires an engineering degree and you are trained in classical music; your upcoming marriage is based on your penchant for charming men rather than on shared love, compatibility, and life goals)?

Or is your fear more general and harder to pinpoint? If so, I invite you to examine what your fear may be revealing:

- Is it possible that you feel this way every time a great opportunity arises because you believe every change to the status quo is dangerous?

- Do you see yourself as an inherently flawed individual who is destined to come up short in every situation?

- Are you convinced that your strong suit is your ability to turn a perfect situation into a mess?

- Do you see yourself failing even before you begin?

Although fear-based misgivings often masquerade as legitimate concerns, at their root, they are tied to something much deeper—the sense that *who you are* is somehow not right—the unspoken belief that you are damaged goods and everything you touch becomes tainted.

This is the posture of *shame*. (See Chapter 2.) While certain fears affect specific areas of our lives, the toxic effects of shame are not compartmentalized. Shame permeates all aspects of our being.

Shame can be compared to yeast that is added to a lump of dough; it affects the entire lump and cannot be separated from it. It causes a physical change to the dough so that the bread rises uniformly. Hence the expression, "A little leaven leavens the whole lump."[1]

In their insightful book, *Dynamics of Power*, Gershen Kaufman and Lev Raphael provide a powerful description of shame and its outflow:

> Shame is the most disturbing experience individuals ever have about themselves; no other emotion feels more deeply disturbing because in the moment of shame the self feels wounded from within. The disturbance produced by shame affects not only self-esteem but also the development of identity and the pursuit of intimacy. Self-esteem, identity, and intimacy are three important dimensions of psychological health which are profoundly influenced by the experience of shame, particularly when it is repetitive or prolonged....By way of definition, to experience shame is to feel *seen* in a painfully diminished sense.[2]

The "diminished sense" mentioned above suggests *inferiority*. To say that something is *inferior* is to imply a comparison with something or someone thought to be *superior*.

When I experience shame, I am making a negative value judgment, not about what I do, but about *who I am*. But shame can become so deeply rooted that judgment can be made in the absence of comparison, as though one's inferiority is a foregone conclusion in every situation.

To feel shame is to perceive yourself as unacceptable and believe that something about you—often the very thing that makes you remarkable—is unacceptable. You will instinctively hide the shame-producing feature from sight, because hiding will be seen as your only hope of receiving acceptance, from others or from yourself.

Too often we accept the burden of shame because we don't realize that we can choose to do otherwise.

THE BIG DISCONNECT

Once the shame-based identity is entrenched, we become fragmented, always working to cover up what we believe to be our shame-producing features. Behind created masks, we become disconnected from ourselves, increasingly self-conscious, and painfully tentative.

In his book, *The Psychology of Shame*, Gershen Kaufman says this about the effects of shame: "Self-consciousness is a manifestation of shame.... We become *self-conscious*, as if the self suddenly were impaled under a magnifying glass."[3] Because the individual living with shame feels overly scrutinized, transparency and spontaneity become off-limits. These healthy traits become too risky, too likely to reveal supposed defects.

Shame-based attitudes also cause us to unplug from people and from life in general. We are unable to be there for others because we cannot show up for ourselves. We expend too much time and energy managing the mask. We deplete the emotional resources that would otherwise be available for activities that promote enjoyment, personal growth, professional advancement, and relational health.

The effects of shame are pervasive. According to Kaufman, "Shame wounds not only the self, but also a family, an ethnic or minority group within a dominant culture, or even an entire nation."[4]

> I submit that there is a global nation burdened with a shame-based identity. The citizens of that nation are the world's women. My mission is to change its face from shame to honor!

Shame is also a relentless taskmaster pressing us into greater dimensions of hiding and demanding the creation of new, improved masks behind which we can hide. Each day the question arises: *Which version of me am I to reveal in this situation?*

The extent of this exercise in futility varies. For some, admission to an elite social circle offers relief from shame. For others, inclusion in an exclusive profession is the answer. In every case, the person dealing with shame works hard to create the impression that they have it all together. They become so skilled at pretending that others believe the mask.

These exhausting façades are designed to make shame-afflicted individuals feel better about themselves and trick others into thinking more highly of them. In reality, façades only deepen the emotional disconnect and lead to an increased sense of isolation.

This is the process by which I became a *strong person hiding*. I was born strong, but I saw strength as being shameful. It started with a misbelief about strength and power that played on the big screen of my mind (and which I accepted as truth):

The people I know mishandle power; therefore, power is a negative. People use their strength to control others. Therefore, the strength with which I was born must be restrained and concealed.

In an effort to differentiate myself from those I saw as abusers of strength, I used my strength to hide my strength. Instead of using it against others, I wielded it against myself. Where others displayed strength by overstepping boundaries, I used strength to keep from defining healthy boundaries of my own. I did this so well that I failed to command my own space; I failed to live life to the fullest.

With my identity so well disguised and my dependence upon others so complete, I believed I could breathe only when they breathed. I could smile only when they smiled. When they got upset, then I chose to be upset. My entire life was built upon illusion and dependency.

Ironically, when we play God in this way, our fabrications of self are more deeply flawed than the authentic self we rejected. Masks cause us to be less accessible to the genuine love and acceptance we crave. Our shame-driven behaviors lead, not to the relief we desire, but to increased suffering.

Don't misunderstand me. The strong person hiding does not want to live in pain; the wounded desire healing. But healing cannot come until we are willing to risk the exposure required to take ownership of a fractured self-image. If we avoid this step to freedom, wholeness remains out of our reach.

GETTING PERSONAL

Like anyone dealing with the effects of shame, I found artificial ways to hold myself together. One of my disguises was an aggressive personality and razor-sharp mouth. Posturing helped me to hide the deep fear I carried within.

In my teen years, the fragments of my life were cobbled together by the rigid structure high school provided. Class schedules, homework assignments, and other activities kept me on rails and gave me a role to play. As long as I stayed in character, I found temporary relief from my mistaken, shame-based identity.

Following graduation, the ruse fell apart. The hallways, walls, and activities that gave me direction dissolved in a moment, and I quickly discovered that I had no internal infrastructure—*no authentic identity*—to sustain me.

Suddenly, my brokenness was exposed. With no place to hide and no mask to wear, I did what millions have done: I became addicted to substances that would literally numb my feelings of inferiority and anesthetize my life.

I lived that way for the next seven years.

Begin to Shatter the Invisible Wheelchair

The emotional wheelchair is constructed of pure, unadulterated, shame-based fear—of rejection, abandonment, and loss.

Emotionally speaking, *acceptance* is the single most compelling need in our lives. That is why its opposites, *rejection and abandonment*, are so painful.

For many, the ultimate rejection is divorce; for others, it is being given up for adoption. Those who have been through either know the searing pain it can produce. No one walks away from these experiences without serious questions about identity.

If being accepted is our most compelling human need and shame reveals the absence of acceptance, then where does healing begin? As a person who found healing from a shame-based identity, I can tell you that wholeness began when I began to accept myself.

I am so thankful for that fateful night when the tide began to turn in my life. It started with a simple choice: I chose to accept God as God, and I chose to accept His love. It was then that I became free to accept and love myself. In turn, I became able to love others.

It started the night I was beaten by my boyfriend. He thrust my head through the windshield of his car and threw me into the gutter. In Chapter 4, I described that moment of pristine clarity; I made an honest assessment of my life. It wasn't pretty. You may recall that I was lying atop a sewer listening to the sound of waste passing below.

How ironic—in some ways the scene was like a snapshot of my life, and I was finally ready to recognize it! I allowed the desperation of my situation to dawn upon me without censoring it or assigning blame to someone else.

Until that night, my life choices were reflected in the condition of that shattered windshield; I could not see where I was going. But that night changed everything; I realized that I was part of creation and as such, an acceptable human being. I understood that I did not have to *become* acceptable or *make myself* acceptable—I simply *was accepted*. Although my invisible wheelchair was not instantly dismantled, it would be in time, because acceptance always brings healing for shame. It is a fundamental human need and necessary for wholeness.

Here are three questions to help you assess your mindset and approach where acceptance is concerned:

1. Do you want to accept yourself for who you are?

2. What is one action you can take to instill within yourself the message that you are acceptable?

3. When you experience rejection (as we all do), how will you respond?

Answer these questions honestly; then consider the following truths relating to acceptance:

- If you believe that all people are created equal, then you are acceptable. Period.

- You can't control the opinions, attitudes, or behaviors of others, but you can choose whether you will internalize their "stuff." If you are accepting of yourself, their opinions will become less consequential to your self-image.

- Contrary to what our emotions might suggest, wholeness and significance are not dependent upon the approval of others. You can choose not to be controlled by those who withhold approval.

Really digest the words of these statements, because only truth can uproot misbeliefs. Shame is *not* a life sentence. You *can* get out of jail and be free.

You hold the key!

A PRACTICAL APPROACH TO MAKING CHOICES ABOUT SHAME

Choice is your greatest asset in shattering the invisible wheelchair. As a life coach working with clients who are dealing with shame, my purpose is never to dredge up pain or discredit life experience. Instead, we enter into a dialogue that invites clients to assess where they are and verbalize where they really want to be.

In this setting, I am attentive to the body language of shame—the lowered face, averted gaze, rounded shoulders. I know that behind that body language there is a *story* that has been spinning in the client's heart and mind, probably for years.

The story—a combination of words and images stored in the memory as it relates to a particular event or experience—is rehearsed in the internal monologue. Clients often attribute their shame to whatever happened in their story. Although events *are* connected to the development of shame, the event itself is typically a side issue. The *real issue* is the unmet need the event exposes.

For the sake of our discussion, let's assume that my client—we'll call him Adam—believes his struggle with shame began with the hurtful words of a parent.

My questions to Adam would be, "Which of your parent's words hurt you? What do those words mean to you? Is that the absolute truth about you, or is it a story you tell yourself—and has this story become a defining narrative in your life?"

Scrutinizing the truth value of hurtful statements by questioning perceptions allows Adam to re-orient himself to a higher viewpoint, design a new outlook, and diminish the power those words have held over him.

The hurtful parental remarks have been captured on Adam's mental video footage and rehearsed for years. Based on his behavior, it is clear that Adam believes he is *getting something* from this memory—whether or not he is cognizant of *what* that is. We tend to return to wells that are producing something we want—whether bitter water or sweet, whether joy or justification of our pain.

The discovery of what is being gained from a hurtful memory affords Adam the ability to make a significant shift in future choices. Therefore, my second question to Adam would be, "What is the story giving you?"

As Adam considers the perceived benefit of rehearsing past events, he is forced to assess their relative importance to his present life. This helps Adam come to terms with any limiting beliefs he may be holding on to. This process can be uncomfortable, yet sticking with it will bring the root—the unmet need—to the surface.

The next question to Adam becomes: "What is the story costing you?" Suddenly, Adam recognizes the price of the story:

- Sleepless nights
- Deteriorating health
- Stagnation at work
- Difficulty in relationships
- Anger
- Rage
- Isolation.

Having identified the perceived gains and apparent losses, Adam quickly realizes that his adherence to the story is not serving him well. He has reached a moment of choice. He is in the driver's seat—not of his past, but of his present and his future—and he is left with two questions to ask himself:

Will I maintain the status quo, and what will that look like?

Will I make a course adjustment, and what will that look like?

For Adam, the status quo has been nothing but painful. Therefore, the cure is attractive. Once Adam believes that circumstances and paradigms are subject to change and *he can change them*, he is free to address, overcome, and lay to rest the events that brought him shame. Adam's history can be rightfully assigned to the past. His emotional attachment to past events can be severed, setting Adam free!

The wheelchair can be sent to the scrap heap—in a million pieces!

To experience choice is to know power. [5]

—Gershen Kaufman

CHECK THE GATE

According to Gershen Kaufman, "Many shame-based individuals...feel as if they are imposters, only waiting to be unmasked."[6] That is the experience of living with a mistaken identity. We fear deep down that the façade will rupture and our worst features will be laid bare.

However, we have a choice about the outcomes of our lives. Therefore, instead of fearing exposure, we can choose to examine the masks we wear, peel them off, and reveal the brilliance of our individuality.

The following interactive steps will help you to expose any cover-ups you have adopted. As you read, fear will exclaim, "Don't go there!" That voice is a clear indication of something hidden. If you're ready to blow your cover, "going there" is exactly what you want to do.

Take time with these points; don't hurry. Move beyond stock responses that may be part of your hiding mechanisms. Place a demand upon yourself for honesty and transparency. Be willing to accept and embrace the person that is revealed, because self-acceptance will force shame to bow its knee and release its grip on your life.

1. Ask three key people in your life to describe their perceptions of you.

    a. Do you respond to their observations with anxiety? joy? suspicion? relief?

    b. To what extent are their descriptions accurate? In what ways do you agree with them?

2. Describe your positive and negative perceptions of yourself in the following areas:

    a. Personality/inner character

    b. Body image

    c. Gifts, talents, strengths

    d. Worth, value

3. Which negative perceptions trigger a sense of shame?

    a. What beliefs, misbeliefs, or outside influences feed this shame?

b. What does holding onto these beliefs/misbeliefs give you?

4. What outcomes are you experiencing as a result of shame? Be specific.

5. What would your life look like if you took ownership of these issues, realigned your thinking with truth, stood tall, and walked out of your invisible wheelchair?

6. What emotions do you feel while answering these questions? Write down your feelings here.

_____

_____

_____

_____

_____

_____

Shame was my identity for so many years, but when the mask came off, healing occurred. Healing is available to you, too. Unlike the superheroes we idolized as children—comic-book creations each possessing a secret identity and a mask—we are at our best when we stand tall in our individuality, commanding (rather than demanding) our own space.

You are invited to choose to remove the mask. In fact, you can unlock any area of your life by using your freedom of choice. Turn the page; we are going to explore your power to choose—and you will discover the vehicle to your dreams!

Chapter 6

CHOICE—THE POWER OF YOUR C.A.R.

WHEN you get in your car, engage the ignition, and put your hands on the steering wheel, you are in command of a vehicle that can take you pretty much anywhere you want to go.

What an analogy for life! When we know what we want and begin to make proactive choices that head in the direction of our dreams, we are firing up the engine that can take us there.

It all starts with the power to choose. However, when our choices become mere reactions, or when we opt *not to choose at all*, the vehicle to our dreams runs out of fuel. The engine sputters and in time, the dream dies. In its place, we are left with a discouraging, draining cycle of disappointing outcomes.

I've been there and done that too many times to count. As is true of anyone who is disengaged from his or her own life, my life eventually became a series of knee-jerk reactions occurring on such a deep emotional level that they were triggered without my conscious awareness or participation. Consequently, I did not fully grasp what was happening to me; nor could I save myself from the emotional tailspin and crash that inevitably followed.

I remember an instance in which I was so unprepared for what transpired as to be completely heartbroken by it. My memory of this experience remains vivid to this day. Ironically, this painful memory is attached to an unforgettable victory in my professional life, one that would be celebrated—not with unceasing joy but with unending tears.

This story began with my dream of becoming a world-class jet-ski racer. From the very first time I witnessed a jet-ski event, I knew I wanted to become a champion in the field. It became my passion; I was certain that I could do it and do it well.

After a lot of hard work, my magic moment came: I broke the existing world record and was deemed the fastest woman in the sport of jet-ski racing. The record I set was a substantial one, the kind that would make any athlete's heart sing. In fact, as of this writing 14 years later, my record remains unbroken.

After that race, although my hands were rendered raw and bloody, I felt like I was on top of the world. The experience was mood elevating in the extreme. My heart was bursting; I felt gratified, thankful, proud, validated, and accepted. It was one of those fleeting moments where the shame *of being* was overshadowed by the rewards *of doing*. Instead of being a forlorn ragdoll, I had become the best version of myself that I could have imagined. I had done my absolute best (a victory in and of itself for someone who had come as far as I had in a few short years!) and received great honor for having accomplished the extraordinary.

My euphoria was short-lived. Just as I was catapulted into the emotional stratosphere, a spokesman for the racing event responded to my achievement with a sentence that crushed me. In a news publication, he characterized my accomplishment simply by saying, "She has done an *unusual* thing" (emphasis mine). In an instant, I plunged from the throne of high achievement to the dungeon of despair.

I remember being stunned as I realized that, of all the available words in the English language, this spokesman had chosen to call my achievement *unusual*. Dozens of laudatory phrases could have described what I had done—and I wanted to hear them all! It had required everything I had in terms of ability, talent, and fortitude—not to mention a healthy dose of divine intervention—to blow through that sporting barrier into the rarefied air breathed only by champions. And all it had amounted to was something that could be labeled and dismissed as *unusual*? Three-legged roosters are *unusual*; but the shattering of a world record deserved to be called *significant!* Or at least it did to me.

At a complete loss for words, I retreated to pit row and cried for what seemed like days. In retrospect, the emotional depths to which I plummeted after the race reflected my misbeliefs (which colored my interpretation of the spokesman's remarks) more than the spokesman's actual words. It wasn't *his voice* that demeaned me; it was the old *voice of shame* interjecting itself into a brand-new situation. There it chanted an old and familiar refrain...

> *You still aren't good enough. You've drawn attention, accolades, trophies, and a world record, but you still are not good enough. Even if you were president of the United States, you wouldn't be good enough.*

WHOSE LIFE IS IT ANYWAY?

In the blink of an eye, *Terri the champion* was demoted back to *Terri the ragdoll*. In reality, I had not been forcibly ejected from the heights; I had abdicated the throne all on my own.

When I heard the word *unusual*, my misbeliefs filtered out any positive content from the spokesman's statement. My shame-based identity triggered and locked onto my default viewpoint—*Terri is never good enough*. This mindset was so deeply ingrained that I subconsciously bypassed the possibility that he was being complimentary.

Even though I didn't consciously realize it, I had chosen to participate, cooperate, and continue in the misbelief that I was not good enough. This choice caused three things to happen:

- I experienced shame in a moment that could have affirmed me.

- I forced positive circumstances to become negative.

- I gave away my power to someone who neither desired nor needed it.

The choices I made in this situation were 100 percent reactive. Sadly, I wasn't aware that I was making these choices, nor was I cognizant that better choices were available. That was precisely the problem. For years I had lived nearly unconsciously; I consistently gave away my personal power to *choose* my thoughts, actions, and outcomes. The choices were mine to make, but I had unwittingly delegated my choices to others.

Although I was not designed to be a ragdoll thrown this way and that by fate, I had never considered the fact that I possessed the authority to make choices that could make a significant difference in my life. *I never stopped to ask myself whether my life was working; I never stopped to ask myself what my life could be like if something were to change. Having given away my power, I had never tried to change anything.*

My life paralleled that of the young girl with the brutish boyfriend. (See Chapter 4.) We had both, by our choices, barricaded ourselves into dead-end situations with no apparent way out. Her insecurities and low self-worth caused her to cling to an unhealthy relationship and mine kept me expecting the worst in every scenario.

Even after an astounding victory in the jet-ski racing event—and the shiny brass ring I hoped would reshape my ailing identity—I gave away my power by allowing someone else's words (or more correctly, my interpretation of those words) to define me. As long as I chose to cling to this misunderstanding, the value of my personal victory would be forever framed by it.

I was at the threshold of opportunity. Instead of the old shattered windshield I'd once looked through, I could choose to see things through a new windshield of opportunity and enjoy this significant achievement; or I could remain confined to the invisible wheelchair that kept me dependent upon others. It was not about the racing spokesman's words, the race, or even building of my reputation as a world-class athlete; this was about *my life,* and I was the only one who could change it.

C. A. R.—The Vehicle to Your Dreams

Beginning in this chapter with our discussion of *choice* and continuing in future chapters, we will explore each of three essential elements required to live the barrier-busting life each of us desires to live.

We'll use an easy-to-remember acronym to facilitate our discussion of what I like to call *the vehicle to your dreams.* Fittingly, the acronym is *C.A.R.* Here's a brief breakdown of what the letters stand for:

C—*Choices.* I base my choices on where I intend to go in life. Figuratively speaking, this is the *windshield* of my C.A.R. Through it, I see my dreams on the horizon. These dreams provide feedback to my decisions so that my choices can be aligned with the outcomes I want to experience.

A—*Actions.* The actions I take breathe life into my decisions and provide backbone, direction, and support for the choices I make. Action is how I follow through on my intentions and get to where I want to go. Actions are the *steering wheel* of my C.A.R.

R—*Results*. These are the outcomes I experience. I continually evaluate my results in light of my stated intentions and objectively assess whether my choices and actions are working for me. If they are not, I give myself permission to change course as often as necessary. Like a driver who assesses changing road conditions, I wisely make *course corrections*, continually adjusting my route until I reach my destination.

THE FUNDAMENTALS OF CHOICE

Let's begin our discussion of choice with an expanded definition of what it means to be *at choice*:

Being *at choice* means that I get to engage proactively with life and with my own heart so that I can participate, cooperate, and be an active part of the decisions and events that shape my life. What I believe, what I want, and what I say matters. I am free to be me!

To fully understand the power and impact of choice, let's examine each element of this working definition more closely.

I get to engage proactively with life and with my own heart. I am privileged (free to choose) to be present at every moment of my life, always "in the game" as opposed to watching from the sidelines. I needn't wait for stuff to hit the fan before I take action; nor must I wait for someone to ratify my personal authority to make choices.

I am not biding my time or hoping for someone to make my decisions for me. I am not retreating from the issues in my life in the hope that someone will rescue me or become my means of escape. *I choose* to seize the moments of my life, and *I choose* to remain connected with my own values, dreams, and desires.

I can participate, cooperate, and be an active part of my life through the decisions, actions, and events that shape my life. This is my life; therefore, I am the one most empowered to affect it—through the actions I choose to take and the ways in which I participate and cooperate with what is best for me. I experience outcomes that are birthed in my desires and that find fulfillment through my choices.

What I believe, what I want, and what I say matters. I am a full-fledged, high-value human being created to contribute in unique and productive ways—to my family, society, and others. Therefore, the beliefs and desires *I choose* are powerful and able to frame an environment in which I can produce results consistent with my unique purpose.

I am free to be me. The fact of my existence proves that I was created as a unique individual. Regardless of the circumstances surrounding conception, no human being is a mistake or accident of nature. My worth is not established through comparison or contrast to others; my worth is inherent in my having been created. *I choose* to be free, and I am only truly free when I become satisfied to be my authentic self.

Everything that is really great and inspiring is created by the individual who can labor in freedom.[1]

—Albert Einstein
Out of My Later Years

WHAT DO YOU WANT?

The ability to make choices is central to being human. Regardless of past experiences, in spite of past errors in judgment or negative outcomes, despite the hurtful things others have said to or about us, we remain at choice. However, making informed, proactive choices means first knowing what you want and then allowing your desire to motivate you to achieve it.

If, like me, you have been a strong person hiding, then achieving a desired outcome begins with the choice to be an agent of change in your own life. You can change anything—perceptions, mindset, decisions, lifestyle, and even your world.

To create the future you long to live, you must have a clear picture of your future in your heart. Often, in pondering the course of our lives, we put the proverbial cart before the horse. Instead of first deciding *what* we want, we worry about *how* and *where*.

But when you know what you want, you are more apt to identify the pathways leading to your desired destination. You will more easily discern the choices that serve your purpose, and you will be positioned to focus on what is important. You will become actively engaged and able to participate and cooperate with your life's goals. Your steps will no longer be random; instead, they will be ordered and intentional.

When you know what you want, you will be better able to sift the wheat from the chaff in every area of your life. You won't be boondoggled by time-wasters and self-sabotage.

For example, if you desire to have a strong marriage, you will choose activities and behaviors that support a healthy relationship, and you will develop a healthy relationship with *self*, which is where all relationships begin. You will also avoid behaviors that weaken your marriage, such as bickering, infidelity, and self-centeredness.

If you want to succeed in your workplace, you will choose to be prompt, respectful, helpful, and supportive. By implication, you will not want to be chronically late, impertinent, uncooperative, or disloyal.

Knowing what you want and what you don't want is the first rung of the choice-making ladder. If I claim to want a strong marriage but choose to flirt with my co-workers, my stated desires will be overwritten by my contradictory actions. Anytime you find a discrepancy between your results and your dream, examine your choices and ask yourself two key questions I ask my life-coaching clients:

1. How are your choices working for you?

2. What would your life look like if you made a change?

These questions serve as gentle but firm reminders that we always have multiple options available to us. We get to make the call, and we can change our minds at any time. That's the beautiful thing about being at choice—if something is not working, you can change it. You are in charge. Just call a time-out, reset the game clock, and choose again!

THREE STEPS TO CHOICE

1. Be *aware* of what is or isn't working for you.

2. Be *willing* to consider another perspective.

3. Back up your stated desires; *accept* the work it takes to achieve them.

GETTING PERSONAL

There is a phrase that I use to remind myself that no situation is hopeless. The words are simple: *Every fact of my life is subject to change.*

These words may sound too good to be true or too Pollyanna-ish to be genuine, yet they *are true,* and my real-life experience bears them out. My life and the facts surrounding my life have turned 180 degrees. More importantly, if the facts of *my* life are subject to change, the facts of *your* life are also subject to change!

Although I'm getting better and better at making good choices, I can remember when all of my choices were bad ones. In fact, when I was a drug addict, my life was nothing more than one bad choice followed by another. I dug a hole so deep that I couldn't find even a kernel of hope that things could get better. After a while, I quit hoping for anything at all.

A part of my life's mission is to uncover the deception of hopelessness and help others to live in freedom. When we believe there is no hope, we are deceived. There is always hope, because there is always another choice we can make. If we'll make even the tiniest decision in support of a better life, hope will begin to percolate inside us and *the facts of our lives will begin to change*!

TO CHOOSE OR NOT TO CHOOSE, THAT'S THE REAL QUESTION

Without the ability to choose, there can be no freedom. And yet, unless we *choose to make choices*, we are imprisoned, just like the slaves who remained confined when they were no longer bound by chains. Similarly, we can allow ourselves to become so emotionally attached to the past that we *refuse to choose* to take advantage of the freedom that beckons.

As we consider the slaves' story on an intellectual level, it is easy to think, *I would never do that. If I were given the choice between freedom and slavery, I would choose freedom every time!* Yet, when you consider your personal history, can you say in all honesty that, during every day and in every situation, you have chosen freedom, without fail?

Speaking for myself, I have not chosen freedom in every circumstance. During the darkest days of my life, I had many opportunities to choose freedom, yet I failed to make that choice. Most of the time, I made no choice at all. As a result, I served a longer sentence in my invisible wheelchair than necessary.

There is a point that I want to make abundantly clear: *Failing to choose is choosing to fail.* My nonchoices were as devastating as my wrong choices. I allowed fear to keep me emotionally paralyzed to the degree that I forfeited my freedom to choose altogether. My limp was manifested in my unwillingness to take a stand for what I believed—about life, about relationships and situations, and about the world.

Zombie-like, I lived in the dead zone of inaction. I accepted the status quo, even when it was killing me. I collapsed under the weight of my self-imposed pressure to please others. I succumbed to the need to be a superwoman who could do it all, and in record time. I caved in to shame and accepted the idea that I was not good enough. I allowed fear to be my master, and I hid from the opportunities I desired most. Instead of engaging proactively in the affairs of my life, I behaved as though I were a pawn in someone else's chess game. I failed to choose actions that honored my being, and I reaped the whirlwind of not being honored by others.

Yes! There came a day when I finally decided to *choose.* By the grace of God, I found acceptance, not because I was all cleaned up, but because I was a human being. This acceptance did not come from others; it came from within and empowered me to envision a new kind of life. Soon, the old ways of *being* and *doing* began to infringe upon this new vision, and I was faced with new choices to be made. These choices could put to rest the old voice of shame and raise new hopes for the future.

At first, my new choices were few and far between and created inner conflict, but every time I saw old and new paradigms colliding, I asked myself whether the old life of hiding was working for me. The answer was always *no!*

That doesn't mean I never took a backward step. Mistakes and misgivings are part of the process of turning your life around. Give yourself permission to make honest mistakes; after all, you are human. Just determine that those experiences will be instructive and formative and that you will keep moving in a positive direction.

The good news is, the further you venture from the place of slavery, the easier it gets to make good choices. The battle to come out of hiding is won incrementally—choice by choice. Each time we resist cover-ups and engage our freedom to choose, even in the smallest of ways, we release the powerhouse within. That powerhouse is the convergence of the mind, the will, and the emotions upon a new way of living...a lifestyle that we are no longer willing to forfeit...a life with which we choose to engage and for which we are willing to change.

Every choice made is an opportunity seized; every choice overlooked is an opportunity discarded.

Far better it is to dare mighty things, to win glorious triumphs even though checkered by failure, than to rank with those poor spirits who neither enjoy nor suffer much because they live in the gray twilight that knows neither victory nor defeat.[2]

—Theodore Roosevelt

CHOOSE TO REDEFINE YOURSELF

When you catch a glimpse of a new and better life with healthier, more productive, and more satisfying outcomes, it gives you a new point of view. If you choose to pursue that new point of view or paradigm, you are accepting an invitation to redefine yourself.

The old you with the old internal monologue, the old misbeliefs, the old living-life-on-the-sidelines mentality, and the ill-fitting disregard for self, cannot travel with you to promising new horizons. The dilapidated self-image that was suitable for hiding won't fit when you step out into the light.

Do you remember the late Rodney Dangerfield, the well-known comedian with the woebegone expression and rumpled tie? Dangerfield built his career on a punch line of sorts; the line was, "I don't get no respect." This trademark won him a tremendous following; almost everyone could relate to his downcast character in one way or another.

For decades, Dangerfield delivered self-deprecating but hilarious quips and anecdotes describing painful experiences of rejection and abandonment. His character was rejected by *everyone*, including his mother. His pitiful expression and nervous tugs on his tie triggered sympathetic laughter from audiences everywhere.

Imagine for a moment a Rodney Dangerfield type of character who has decided to transform his life and develop a new sense of self-respect. Now imagine that, everywhere he goes on his quest for significance, he continues to say, with his same sad expression, "I don't get no respect."

Even as an analogy, the scenario is absurd. Yet, the principle remains: If I desire to change my life in a significant way, then I have accepted the invitation to redefine myself—not by compulsion, but because it serves my purpose. It stands to reason that if I continue to define myself as someone who gets no respect, then respect is the last thing I can expect to receive.

When I recall the meaning I ascribed to the well-intended comments of the racing spokesman about the speed record I'd set, it is clear that I was still hiding in my ragdoll persona. Until I decided that *ragdoll* was not my identity, I would necessarily continue to walk out a ragdoll's existence.

To break free, I needed to embrace and project the authentic Terri, check my emotional posture (the gait we talked about in Chapter 2), and ask myself the following questions:

- Does my posture reflect the authentic me I choose to be?

- What choices do I need to make in order to achieve the outcomes I desire?

When you choose to redefine yourself, you do it on a variety of levels. Words, actions, attitudes, appearance—all are subject to change. But it all begins with choices. Here is a short list of the kinds of choices we can make in order to redefine ourselves and shed an inauthentic identity:

- We can choose to commit to change.

- We can choose to become focused.

- We can choose to change our focus.

- We can choose to take the quality time necessary to cause a change in our lives for the better.

- We can choose to break free of unwanted roles and mistaken identities.

- We can choose to love ourselves.

This list is by no means comprehensive. You may want to reread it and consider the choices you would add that are more specific to your quest for freedom.

CREATE THE BOUNCE

Let's get specific about choice by creating the bounce in the area of rejection. When we feel rejected, being at choice frees us to decide whether we will internalize the bitterness of rejection and be defined by it, or process the experience in an intentional manner so we can move forward.

Think back to the last time you suffered from a significant rejection experience and ask yourself the following questions. Commit your answers to writing and then read your answers aloud so you can hear them. As your inner thoughts are verbalized, ask yourself what is driving your responses.

1. What does this rejection really mean to me, and how does it affect or play out in my life?

2. Am I truly being rejected by another person, or have my misbeliefs contributed to this experience? How?

3. Do I reject myself, and do I expect to be rejected?

4. Is there an unmet need underlying this experience of rejection? What is the nature of the unmet need, and what would I name it?

5. What choices can I make in responding to feelings of rejection? How might these choices alter future outcomes in my life?

When you make a choice, you are effectively taking a stand—for what you want, for what you believe, for what is right. Being at choice is empowering and invites you to take ownership of your life. Taking responsibility in this way opens the door to healing, and healing frees you to act confidently and experience enhanced results. When that happens, your new, improved life—your life of freedom—is just around the corner!

Chapter 7

ACTION PUTS
YOUR C.A.R. IN MOTION

Men acquire a particular quality by constantly acting a particular way... you become just by performing just actions, temperate by performing temperate actions, brave by performing brave actions.[1]

—Aristotle

ARISTOTLE'S use of the word *men* as the subject of this quote might appear to be politically incorrect in our contemporary world, yet his clear message adds an important twist to our earlier premise that beliefs give rise to actions. Our beliefs *do inform* our actions, but we still get *to choose* what we will do. When we choose actions that support increasingly positive outcomes, our actions can *transform us*!

On the Hollywood set, my actions as a stuntperson can determine whether I and my coworkers go home in one piece at the end of the day. In fact, depending upon what I do or fail to do, one or more of us might not go home *at all*. It is an analogy for life—wise choices, careful preparation, and thorough execution of the plan have everything to do with the results we achieve, and these results affect, not only the way things turn out, but who we become.

Doing is not the same as *being*, but *doing affects being*. The actions you take can transport you from one place, or one state of mind, to another. Think back to your first day of school. You were probably nervous about going. You may have experienced a sense of dread, but you faced your fear and worked your way through it. Before long, your fears about going to school dissolved. As a result, you not only received an education, but you also developed the ability to acclimate to change and to expand your horizons. You took the risks associated with a specific action and *your doing affected your being*.

The same dynamic operates in stunt work. There's a stunt experience I'll never forget. My job was to stand on top of an 80-story building. If you don't have a specific fear of heights, standing still atop tall buildings sounds easy enough. However, the director's instructions complicated things just a little; he told me to stand there and "look natural."

That's easier said than done! I quickly discovered that standing still and looking "natural" while poised hundreds of feet above the concrete pavement required a lot more energy than I had imagined it would. In fact, it would have been easier for me to jump from eighty stories than to stand still and pretend to be unaffected.

I call this stunt experience *the edge*. It reminds me of those extreme moments in life when I have sensed myself teetering on the verge of something new and unknown. In those moments, I often feel uneasy, sometimes even fearful, like so many children do on that first day of school.

When I'm standing on the brink in this way, I can *choose* to remain frozen in place. This choice requires no action of me; it is what I would call *default mode*. It offers me relative safety (I say *relative safety* because the chance of falling remains). Although I'm taking no specific action, default mode does exact a price in the sense that I must expend energy in order to maintain my balance, cover up my fear, and wear my "natural" mask.

I've learned that the more productive choice is for me to engage proactively with the situation. When I choose to do so, I am able to transform the scary edge on which I am perched into a *launch pad*. From there, I can blast off into the realm of opportunity, a place where I can flourish and grow. I am fully aware that risk will be present there; I can't control every factor, and my journey won't be perfect...but it will be alive with freedom.

C.A.R.—"A" Is for *Action*

Remember, the C.A.R. to your dreams has three parts. In Chapter 6, we discussed the first element, which is *choice*. When we make choices, we fire up the engine of the vehicle of our dreams. Once the engine is running, we have the opportunity to follow through on our choices by placing our hands on the steering wheel and *driving*.

This combination of *choice* and *action* is the difference-maker when it comes to outcomes. You are the one who gets to choose which way you will go in life and which actions will take you there. If you fuel your actions with intentionality, the making of specific choices for specific reasons, your steps will consistently lead you in the direction of your dreams.

First, evaluate how your life is going so far. If you feel as though your goals are moving out of your reach, retrace your steps. Are your actions (and for that matter, your choices) lining up with your desired outcomes, or have you begun to veer off your intended pathway? It is true that action produces movement, but not all movement supports your stated goals.

Or do you feel stuck in a rut? If so, identify the point at which you stopped moving forward. You may discover it is the same point at which you retreated from making choices and taking appropriate action. In other words, you may find that you have been frozen on *the edge*. Don't bemoan your past lack of action or loss of time—just restart your engine and get moving!

"THE HAVES" AND "THE HAVE NOTS"

At one time or another, each one of us has experienced the feeling that life is passing us by. You may have suffered a marital, financial, or physical setback. You might feel as though your life never really got on track in the first place. Either way, you can end up feeling left behind, as though the world and everyone in it were moving forward without you.

Think of the people whom you consider to be great. We'll call them *the Haves*. Whether they are presidents, astronauts, artists, or war heroes, their stories speak highly of them. We see them as being the cream of the crop, an esteemed group in a class all their own. It is easy for us to assume that accomplished men and women have been magically endowed with the "right stuff" because it is obvious that *something* has set them apart from the rest of us.

Our perception is at least partially accurate: in terms of achievement, great men and women are thought of as being great because they have accomplished what few would even dare to attempt.

Where many of us deceive ourselves is in terms of our own potential; we tend to see ourselves as being unable or unqualified to achieve at the lofty level of our heroes. We see ourselves as *the Have Nots* because we don't always recognize within ourselves the potential to do great things.

If we believe that others are built for greatness while we are destined for mediocrity, we are deceived. Greatness has always been about ordinary people doing extraordinary things. If we could peer inside the private lives of our heroes, we would discover that they face the same struggles we do; they are just as insecure and vulnerable as we are.

There is a mere hairsbreadth of difference separating *the Haves* from *the Have Nots*. The difference is that those whom we admire decided at some point, and remained committed thereafter, to press through dislikes, difficulty, and fear in order to persist in their endeavors. They *chose* to *act* in a manner consistent with their goals, knowing that although failure, embarrassment, and rejection were distinct possibilities, success and fulfillment were also achievable. By accepting risk and taking action, these men and women have left their mark on the world, benefiting themselves and others.

One such figure was Fred Astaire. As a child, Astaire danced with his sister, Adele. The pair performed on the vaudeville circuit and were considered among the best child performers of their day. Fred, who was seen as the less talented of the siblings, persevered in spite of his perceived shortcomings. He continued working to develop his gifts as a dancer and singer and learned to play several instruments.

In time, Fred's skill exceeded Adele's. The two continued as partners and moved from vaudeville to Broadway. Hoping to break into motion pictures, they auditioned for Paramount Studios, whose executives saw nothing particularly promising in the Astaires' presentation and rejected the dance duo. Fred's solo screen test for RKO Studios was also disappointing; his often-quoted test results were reported to have read as follows: "Can't act. Slightly bald. Can dance a little"![2]

In time, Adele married and retired from show business. At first, Fred saw his sister's retirement as a setback, but he turned it into an opportunity to expand his horizons. He went on to have a legendary career in music, dance, and film and remains one of the premier names in the entertainment industry. Dance icons Balanchine and Nureyev are said to have regarded Astaire as the world's greatest dancer![3]

Successful living begins with the choices we make and continues with the actions we take. When we persistently choose actions that harmonize with our desired outcomes, those actions can bring the results for which we long.

Well-chosen actions not only change the circumstances around us, they also transform us from within by causing us to develop into the people we were created to be. Over time, our actions can transport us from the constricting domain of *the Have Nots* into the wide-open, sunny world of *the Haves*.

> *Don't be too timid and squeamish about your actions. All life is an experiment. The more experiments you make the better.*[4]
>
> —Ralph Waldo Emerson

QUESTION YOUR FEARS

When fear grips your soul, how do you respond? Do you automatically interpret fear as a signal to retreat...or do you become more determined to advance toward your goal?

This is a loaded question because, if you're like most people, your past experiences can cause a knee-jerk response that says, *Fear couldn't possibly be a signal for anything but retreat!*

Well, yes...and no. Certain healthy fears, such as the fear of touching a hot iron, stepping in front of a moving train, or jumping out of an airplane without a parachute, dictate retreat, and with good reason. If you go forward with any of those activities, you're going to get hurt, and you could lose your life.

However, many other fears are triggered when *false evidence appears real*. More often than we realize, our fears of failure, rejection, and embarrassment are based not directly upon our past experiences but on the misbeliefs we have formed as a result of those experiences.

This kind of fear response tricks us into retreating from life's greatest opportunities and trains us to seek counterfeit forms of safety, hiding places where we believe we can take shelter and avoid repeat performances of painful events.

If you will question your fears, your life will change dramatically. It is a matter of putting fear to the truth test by asking, Are these feelings of fear a healthy response to legitimate danger, or are they based upon a misperception that serves only to threaten my advancement? Are these fears signaling a wise retreat, or should I override them and continue in my advance?

When fear grips your heart, you remain *at choice*. Depending upon how accurately you appraise the legitimacy of your fear and how you choose to respond based on that appraisal, you will either experience a breakthrough or come to a deadening standstill. Whether you are ready to believe it or not, fear can be a signal to advance!

THE DOOR OF FEAR

Let's begin with this statement: *Courage is not the absence of fear, but the decision to act in spite of, and in the presence of, fear.* Without fear, courage is not possible. Show me someone who is admired for his or her bravery and I will show you someone who has felt fear breathing down his or her neck.

Courage is a choice. It waits in the wings for us to engage it, and when we do, the courage rises up within us. The key to having courage is found in how you "hold" or handle your fear.

There is a visualization exercise that has been helpful to me and to my clients. In this exercise, fear is pictured as a being a door. The door of fear has a knob or handle; this doorknob represents the ability and the opportunity to open the door.

When I approach the door of fear, I can choose to see it one of two ways—as an obstacle or as an entryway. My attitudes toward fear will dictate my choice. If I assume that fear is to be avoided at all costs and all fears signal retreat, then I will see the door of fear as an obstacle and the door will remain closed. I may not know what is on the other side of the door, but whatever it is, I have decided that I cannot or will not reach it or even see it.

Enter the power of courage. If I suspend fear long enough to examine the situation more carefully, I will be reminded that a door is *not* a wall. A wall is fixed, but a door is designed to provide access to whatever is behind it. If access to that space is useless or harmful, there would be a wall in front of us—not a door.

If I engage courage and reach for the door knob, it will allow me to *handle* my fear so that I can *use* the door to serve my purpose. When I turn the knob, I access the opportunity waiting on the other side.

This is important to my overall outcomes because opportunities are not happenstance. In fact, they are often providential. Opportunities are stepping stones to the next level in my life. Through the opportunities I encounter and engage, I am able to advance toward my dreams and my destiny.

When we choose to engage courage, we are free to take action. Instead of fleeing from challenges, we are able to accurately assess our circumstances and determine to move through them. It is as though we were to turn the door handle of opportunity with one hand and insert the key of courage with the other. This dual action, if consistently applied in the presence of fear, has the power to launch us into the world of *the Haves*.

GET REAL WITH FEAR

When fear strikes, don't pretend you aren't afraid. Being in denial about fear is to deny yourself the opportunity to gain ascendancy over it. Acknowledge your fear; be curious about it and begin to ask yourself probing questions:

1. In the face of fear, what is my first impulse? Escape? Avoidance? Aggression?

2. When was the last time I reacted to fear in any of these ways?

3. How else is my fear showing up? Does my neck tighten? Do I suffer from a queasy stomach or an aching head?

4. What can I gain from these experiences?

TWIN EMOTIONS: FEAR AND EXCITEMENT

I remember the first time I rode a jet ski. I rocked and wobbled every which way. If you had been watching me from the shore, you would never have guessed that I had the potential to become a champion jet-ski racer.

It is frightening to ride a jet ski when you don't have a sense of control over the machine, and rightly so. Jet-ski accidents can be deadly. Yet, because I had in mind a vision of becoming a champion jet-ski racer, I continued my quest to ride. I decided to contend with fear and with the quirks of the machine and gain control of both. Even in my state of diminished self-worth, I arrived at the conclusion that I could hold my fear in such a way as to use it to serve my purpose.

The equation was simple: I simply could not become a champion jet-ski racer without passing through the door of fear. Had I opted to see the door as a signal to retreat, someone else would have broken the world record, and I would have asked myself "What if?" questions, maybe for rest of my days.

How much would it have cost me in terms of personal and professional development and the realization of my dreams? The answer is, *potentially everything.*

The issue always comes back to how you handle fear. Physiologically speaking, the body responds to fear and excitement in the same ways: the pulse quickens, adrenaline flows, the palms get sweaty, we rise to a state of full alert, and we become completely focused on the task at hand.

The central nervous system does not distinguish between fear and excitement. We are the ones who label our experiences. We call an event *exciting* based on a positive appraisal of the situation. Yet, we could label identical circumstances *frightening* if we perceive them to portend negative implications.

Walt Disney and Universal Studios get this formula. Elaborate amusement parks are built all over the world for precisely this reason: the extreme ride that is greatly feared by some people is highly sought after by others who perceive it as an adventure. Disney and Universal know that thrill-seekers are willing to *pay money* in exchange for the experience.

You are wired to experience the physiological changes brought on by the twin emotions of fear and excitement. The neurological mechanisms are built into your physical being. Therefore, unless there is some mitigating physical condition, your responses to fear and excitement will occur spontaneously; you do not have to "work up" your reactions.

Still, there is at your command a switch that governs your emotional response to this physiological power source: You can flip the switch from *fear* to *excitement* and back again based on your perception of the situation at hand.

It's similar to the electrical wiring in your home. You use electricity to refrigerate your food, but you can also use it to heat the oven. The electricity doesn't care how it is used; it will accomplish whatever you ask of it.

The same thing is true of your physiological and emotional wiring. You can decide to use these responses to serve your advantage because you have the power to flip the switch. Depending upon the choice you make, the fear/excitement response mechanism can help you to achieve your desired outcomes or it can keep you frozen on the cusp of something better.

Once you decide how to hold fear to your advantage, you can harness the energy it produces and apply it to positive action. You are then free to accurately assess the risk/reward balance sheet presented by each opportunity that comes your way. Because your assessments are not fear-based, you will be able to fling open the doors of opportunity, live the life you choose, and enjoy life more. You will quickly discover that having power and using it is better than giving it away.

There may be times when you will have to kick down the door of fear using courage as your battering ram. Do it! Mastering fear takes a conscious effort; you have to stand up and walk through it. Otherwise, fear will master you and you won't consciously realize it.

TURN YOUR FEAR INTO POWER

Get proactive with fear. Instead of *reacting*, become curious about it; be open to different ways of seeing it. Inspect your fear from a variety of angles. Find a way to use it to your advantage. Decide that it is okay to be nervous and take action anyway.

Use the adrenaline. Embrace the energy. Embrace the physical rush fear causes. Loosen up. Breathe. Smile. Adjust your point of view until you recognize the opportunity that is waiting behind the door of fear. See yourself as the predator rather than the prey—and then pounce.

GETTING PERSONAL

The day I set the jet-ski race record was an exciting day—to the max! The energy generated by the competition was so high and the momentum created by that energy was so profound that I thought of nothing but putting my fastest time in the record books.

My hands were raw and bloody, but it didn't matter. The experience of being present to the moment, both to the intricacies of the slalom course and to the opportunity the event provided, was all that mattered. I was poised on the threshold of a dream, and I decided to ride that jet ski straight to my destiny.

As I stared at the starting gate of the 275-foot slalom course, I waited for the moment that I would blast through the entrance gate to start the time clock.

With the jet-ski rocketing underneath me, slicing the water and turning with precision as I negotiated the first turn, I carved hard and flew through the next fifty feet to the second turn. Looking ahead of the curve, I saw the third turn and the turnaround buoy up ahead.

That's when something indescribable happened. I felt myself split into two as if I were participating in the event *and* watching from somewhere above my being. This sensation continued until the end of the race when I looked over to the posting clock and saw the notation, "23:04—A New World Record!" With water dripping down my face, I blinked my eyes repeatedly to be sure I was seeing the clock correctly.

People were yelling and jumping in excitement. I was shaking inside with amazement that I had accomplished precisely what I had set out to do. At the time, it seemed as though I had achieved everything that I could possibly hope to finish in a lifetime. Thankfully, there was much more to come!

ACTION IS A TRANSFORMING EXPERIENCE

Aristotle was spot on; the actions we take have the potential to change us from within. When you choose courage, the actions you complete will cause you to become brave. When you choose to be self-disciplined, your actions will create a lifestyle or habit of diligence.

Completing the dream of being the fastest woman in the history of the sport of jet-ski racing was a significant undertaking for me. Because of my damaged self-image and emotional issues, I had always been prone to giving up before I started. (You'll remember that I was a strong woman who thought it was shameful to use her strength, therefore I did not apply my strengths. Instead, I surrendered every cause before I had to ante up with my personal power.)

After breaking the world record, I believed I could do *anything*. My mind-set had changed; instead of sporting a defeatist mentality, I rediscovered the threads of hope within me and began to access the will to overcome adversity.

I was no longer a bystander. Instead, I was an active participant in the race of life. No longer would I need to rely on anyone else to take the jump for me. I didn't need to be rescued or to cast blame on others. It seemed as though my Creator was speaking to me through these events, saying, "You are so valuable to Me. I have recorded time and inscribed your name on it."

Suddenly, my grey world burst into Technicolor. My dreams became tangible, because I believed I could achieve them. I was committed to getting done whatever needed to be done in order to break out of the box I had lived in for so long. I disciplined every fiber of my being to cooperate with the plan to release and fulfill my potential in life.

The change that had begun on that dark night in the gutter after my head was thrust through the windshield (long before I became a stuntperson who would do that for a living!) was continuing to bear fruit in my life. One choice birthed another; each action kicked down another door. Freedom came incrementally, and I learned to grasp its power with increasing confidence over time.

Racing taught me many meaningful lessons. Most importantly, it taught me what courage is. (Since then, my work as a stuntwoman has taught me what fear is not, and has revealed the wide gulf separating fearlessness from the performance of fearless acts.)

Among the things I have learned about courage are three fundamental truths:

1. Courage is only genuine when fear is present.

2. Courage means feeling the effects of fear and choosing to advance anyway.

3. Courage means getting up again, no matter what.

Racing compelled me to choose life-transforming actions. These actions revised my approach to life itself. I learned to pay the price for what I wanted, and I learned to align my choices with the precise actions designed to unleash my desired results. I am living proof that transformation is possible—for each of us.

Consider this your invitation to get in the C.A.R., take the steering wheel, and *drive.*

CHECK THE GATE

Let's make sure the information now available to us is fully captured in our hearts and ready to become operational in our lives.

Consider a situation in which you are currently standing on *the edge.* Allow your curiosity free reign as you acknowledge, assess, and question any fearful thoughts and attitudes. Then allow yourself the freedom to explore alternative approaches to these ideas.

1. Describe the situation under consideration.

2. What emotions arise when you think of this situation?

    a. Are you eager to take action?

    b. Would it feel better to let sleeping dogs lie?

    c.   Who, in your view, are the *Haves* and the *Have Nots* in this situation?

3.   Is this situation exciting or frightening? What is the determining factor in this assessment?

4.   Describe your door of fear in this situation and describe your approach to it. Does the door look more like an obstacle or opportunity?

5.   Which actions are available to you? How might doing affect your state of being if you choose to take action?

If we shrink from the hard contests...then the bolder and stronger peoples will pass us by.[5]

—Theodore Roosevelt

Often the worst step you can take is to take no step at all. If you aren't in motion, there is no force, whether natural or supernatural, that can turn you in the right direction. You and you alone are the key to the rest of your life. You can choose to advance toward your desired outcomes, or you can remain perched and frozen on the brink of your dreams.

The results are yours to determine. We'll unpack *results* in the next chapter.

Chapter 8

RIDE YOUR C.A.R.
TO REWARDING RESULTS

ONE of my most memorable professional experiences was the stunt work I was privileged to perform for the epic Hollywood blockbuster, *Titanic*.

Imagine the gargantuan dimensions of the set: a built-to-scale replica of the *Titanic*, which stood sixty feet tall and included a massive hydraulic system designed to produce the listing of the boat. The hydraulics created phenomenal effects, but they also had the power to send dozens of stuntpersons flying into the air like kernels of human popcorn.

Safety chains were used to minimize the risk of unexpected "launches," but at one point the chains failed! Thankfully, there were no major injuries, but we were left hanging off the side of the boat for ninety minutes. You could say that everyone on the set was feeling the pressure that day.

With the hydraulics in motion, standing on the deck of the boat was challenging. If you have ever entered a slanted room at the amusement park, you know how disorienting it can be to stand on a pitched surface. On the set of

Titanic, we wore the apparel of the day. For the ladies, this included lace-up shoes with tiny lifts.

The shoes certainly added to the overall effect, not only in terms of historical accuracy, but also in terms of the stunt work and special effects. The shoes caused us to slip and slide more easily, so that when the massive ship replica was tilted to create a 20-degree list, we completely lost our footing. Imagine what happened when the list angle was increased to 90 degrees!

During the *Titanic* shoot, we learned a lot about the actual story of the *RMS Titanic.* Although we experienced a fair share of unexpected events on the film set, they were nothing compared to what happened in the tragic real-life drama at sea.

When the *RMS Titanic* embarked on her maiden voyage on April 10, 1912, expectations soared. Those on board looked forward to a magnificent journey on the most luxurious ocean liner of its day. Sadly, the outcome of the journey was far from what anyone imagined. Instead of a stellar inaugural outing on the high seas, the *Titanic* was headed for a one-way journey to the ocean's floor.

Close to midnight on April 14, the *Titanic* struck an iceberg. Within hours, the ship sank, and 1,500 people perished in the icy waters of the North Atlantic. This ghastly event shocked the world. How could the "unsinkable" *Titanic* have been so vulnerable, so utterly doomed?

An inquiry into the shipwreck revealed that the liner was traveling at excessive speeds in treacherous waters. Other circumstances combined to make disaster inevitable: the number of lifeboats was insufficient; the firing of *Titanic's* red rockets, intended to signal distress, were mistaken by nearby vessels for celebratory fireworks; and evacuation of the ocean liner reportedly got off to a late start.

The circumstances of the *Titanic's* demise suggest that the famous maiden voyage could have ended much differently. The tragedy might well have been avoided; however, a happier ending was not to be. At best, many lessons were learned and many were taken to heart.

If such calamitous outcomes were to be avoided in the future, critical procedural changes and structural improvements would be needed. Maritime laws and procedures were revised, and construction standards were raised to ensure greater safety and preparedness on the high seas.

C.A.R.—"R" Is for Results

For the purposes of our discussion, *results* are the outcomes we experience in life. These outcomes are based primarily on the choices we have made and the actions we have taken, although results are sometimes affected by factors beyond our control. Results comprise the third component of the vehicle to your dreams.

Whether or not our results are favorable, they always provide us with opportunities to learn and grow. When our results alarm us, we learn many things, and we learn them quickly. All too often, as in the case of the *Titanic*, we learn them the hard way.

Although undesirable outcomes can be painful, they needn't leave us feeling powerless. On the contrary, we can feel empowered by the much-needed information they provide. When we take this newfound knowledge to heart and act accordingly, we increase the likelihood of improved outcomes in the future.

Consider your personal and professional history. Some of your results probably turned out as you expected—you had a plan in mind, you executed the plan, and your desired outcome was achieved.

More often than we care to admit, our results turn out differently than we expected—sometimes *very* differently. When outcomes catch us off-guard in this way, we have two ways to respond:

1. We can give in to panic, thereby relinquishing our personal power

2. We can take ownership of our results, thereby transforming the setback into a growth opportunity.

When we *own* our outcomes and make appropriate adjustments to our approach, we maintain the upper hand, in large part because our disappointing outcomes are not permitted to define us. We position ourselves in a posture of power, the state of mind of being or becoming a *victor* rather than a *victim*. This state of readiness increases the likelihood that we will gain from and build upon the experience in positive, enriching ways.

From this proactive position, we can objectively examine our results and begin to release ourselves from self-condemning tendencies. We can forgive ourselves for the mistakes we've made, and we can forego the need to blame others. This enables us to focus on more constructive activities. Instead of clinging to the past, we are free to move forward, assess our outcomes in the context of our desires, and make life-enhancing adjustments.

Of course, when outcomes go awry, we tend to experience a range of emotions, some of which challenge our composure. If we will accept the fact that humans and the human experience are imperfect, we will regain our composure more readily. We will be able to remind ourselves that disappointing outcomes—even the most costly ones—can generate our most valuable learning experiences and the greatest opportunities to grow, gain confidence, and hone our professional, relational, intellectual, and practical skills.

PERFECTION IS A PIPEDREAM

Practicing self-acceptance in these situations is not the same as being flippant about our missteps or insensitive to the impact of our blunders upon others. It means that we can pick ourselves up, brush ourselves off, and become part of the solution.

Many things—too many things—went wrong on the *Titanic.* Many lives, both young and old, were lost needlessly. These costly mistakes could have been avoided, but they could never be undone.

Remorse for the deadly mistakes made was fitting, but remorse alone could not produce needed change. Instead of stopping at despair, the experts and authorities who examined the causes of the *Titanic* disaster took innovative steps forward. They pushed for important reforms and higher levels of accountability to secure the safety of seagoing passengers. The course adjustments that resulted from their efforts have enabled countless ocean liners to steer clear of disaster since the dark days of 1912.

Nearly a century later, you might expect that maritime safety would have arrived at a state of perfection in which all accidents at sea could be eliminated. Yet, accidents still occur and will likely continue to happen in the years to come.

Why is this so? The answer is simple: perfection *is* a pipedream. Whether in international travel or any other field of endeavor, we never really *arrive.* Mankind continues to make improvements and seek better ways of doing things, yet it is unreasonable to expect perfect outcomes in every situation. Even if we managed, somehow, to do everything right in every instance, we would eventually encounter circumstances that are beyond our ability to control.

Perfection as a norm is a beautiful dream but an unachievable one. Even when we do our very best and try our hardest, our results can miss the mark.

Thomas Alva Edison learned that firsthand. He performed multiplied tens of thousands of experiments and held nearly 1,100 patents. Yet, most of Edison's efforts did not produce the results he desired or expected. In some circles, the inventor is as well known for his willingness to push past the disappointment of failed outcomes as he is for his outstanding achievements.

Had we been in Edison's shoes, many of us would have interpreted repeated failures as signals to retreat. Edison could have wallowed in despair, quit, or questioned the validity of his calling. Instead, he took his losses in stride and recognized the value wrapped inside his near-misses. Edison knew that as long as he followed his life's dream and steadfastly applied himself to his mission, both his successes and failures would move him closer to the outcomes he was seeking.

Because he persevered, Edison fulfilled his destiny and revolutionized our world. He was a man driven by his cause. He worked eighteen-hour days and derived enormous satisfaction from his work. We, too, derive pleasure from Edison's efforts; among his many accomplishments are the perfection of the incandescent light bulb and the invention of the phonograph, motion picture camera, and fluorescent electric lamp!

Thomas Alva Edison was neither a perfect man nor a perfect inventor. Neither did he expect perfect results. Yet he was one of the most productive individuals of all time. Among the most inspiring elements of Edison's legacy are the life lessons and the example of perseverance he left us!

Results? Why, man, I have gotten lots of results! If I find 10,000 ways something won't work, I haven't failed. I am not discouraged, because every wrong attempt discarded is often a step forward....[1]

—Thomas A. Edison

COURSE CORRECTIONS WELCOMED HERE

How would you rate your life outcomes overall? Do you view your success/failure balance sheet with the sanguine repose that Thomas Edison did? Or does a diminished sense of *self* poison your perspective and over-magnify your failures? When you consider your missteps—yes, even your *blunders*—do you want to throw up your hands in disgust and retreat to the La-Z-Boy with a box of donuts?

If you can't relate to the Thomas Edison approach to failure, ask yourself these questions: What is it about my mistakes that cause me to stay stuck in them? Am I as powerless in this situation as I feel?

If the captain of the *Titanic* could have turned back the hands of time to just before the ship's encounter with the iceberg, he surely would have put 20/20 hindsight to work. He would have swallowed any seaman's pride about his authority, judgment, or ability for a second chance to preserve 1,500 innocent lives.

When we witness the failures of others, we are quick to applaud those who learn from their mistakes and move forward—and we *should* applaud them. Had the *Titanic* captain managed to wrest the ship from the jaws of destruction, he would surely have been hailed as a hero.

Yet, when it comes to our own failures, we are quick to condemn ourselves and to forbid ourselves redemption. Instead, we choose to go down with the ship and remain entombed in the memory of our mistakes.

The more reasonable course of action would be to respect ourselves as much as we do others by giving ourselves permission to make mistakes and overcome them. If we accept our missteps as a natural part of life, we will be able to learn from them; we will also be more open to new ways of looking at things. Then we can follow Edison's example by allowing ourselves room to learn, grow, and make improvements.

Course corrections are a vital part of successful navigation. You are at the helm of your ship and as long as you have breath in your lungs, you can turn your ship around. Your past need not be an indication of your future. *Your results are subject to change!*

A life spent making mistakes is not only more honorable, but more useful than a life spent doing nothing.[2]

—George Bernard Shaw

Vision, Purpose, and Results

You have probably heard the saying, *"If you don't know where you're going, any road will take you there."* When you don't have a particular destination in mind, you will accept and adjust to any place you happen to end up. That doesn't mean that you will be happy or excited to be there; it just means that you'll see one endpoint as being just as good as another, because you had no preference in the first place.

That approach to destiny is reactive and fatalistic. It is the ragdoll mentality with which I lived for years; it is demonstrative of a posture of pain (a victim mentality), which most often produces disappointing results. The hapless ragdoll is subject to the whims of others and ends up wherever it is tossed. *But we are not ragdolls*! We get to choose where we want to go and what we want to accomplish. We were not born to be people of chance, but people of *vision*.

There are many terrific books in print that focus solely on the subjects of vision and purpose. That is not our intention here. However, these topics are important to our discussion of results, so we will explore them below, through brief statements about their qualities.

A compelling vision determines your course. We've talked about the importance of mid-course corrections, but what about having a vision of where you are going in the first place? You not only have the power to change course, you are at choice to establish the course of your life's journey and to do so with intentionality.

The crew of the *Titanic* set sail with the best of intentions. They had specific destinations and a clear travel plan in mind. The fact that the ship sank was not reflective of a lack of vision or direction; instead, the accident occurred due to an inadequate response to changing conditions.

When you have a compelling vision of your destination, you take ownership of that vision by taking three important steps to ensure your desired outcomes:

1. You choose the best path to take you there.

2. You make adjustments to your course to ensure a safe arrival and to produce the greatest benefits along the way.

3. You measure the outcomes you experience by comparing them to your standard, which is the vision that guides your journey.

Your vision is worthy of being articulated. Since your vision determines your course, the value of your vision cannot be underestimated!

For your vision to remain compelling, you need to articulate it. Perhaps the most effective way to articulate your vision is to write it down and to be willing to refine it or rewrite it as necessary. Writing down your vision helps you to see it clearly. The better able you are to visualize your destination, the better your chances of getting there.

Your vision is linked to your purpose. A compelling vision guides and defines your life's outcomes, but what makes your vision compelling in the first place? The answer is *purpose.* When you connect with your life's purpose (to be a mom, a doctor, a journalist, or a gardener, or simply to help others in need) your vision will become clear.

Thomas Edison had a passion for technological progress and a strong sense of purpose. He believed he was called to benefit society by furthering the development of technology. This sense of purpose propelled him forward and sustained his passion through decades of successes and failures.

Your purpose and vision will measure your results. Edison's knowledge of self and mission also enabled him to evaluate his results accurately. He did not *de*value his seemingly failed efforts because he knew it was his job as a scientist and inventor not only to discover what worked but also to uncover the methods that wouldn't work. With each failed experiment, he narrowed down the field of possibilities and often bumped into answers for other unsolved questions. Either way, when weighed in light of his vision, all of Edison's results were useful.

Vision illuminates your values and values, govern your approach to achievement. Your vision reflects who you are. Therefore, when your vision is articulated, it will harmonize with the values you hold dear. There are many ways to arrive at your destination, but not all paths are compatible with your belief system. For instance, if you value integrity, you will not use unethical means to achieve your desired results. Instead, you will govern your choices in line with your values, and your life's purpose will become increasingly clear.

Vision supports attitudes and behaviors that enhance your results. A strong sense of vision will help you sustain your commitment to your life's purpose and help you to maintain the discipline required to achieve consistent results.

Commitment and discipline are the tools you use to build a sturdy bridge from where you are to where you want to be. Disciplines are the daily actions you take in order to maintain steady progress and achieve your desired outcomes. Commitment is the ingredient that will keep you focused when distractions and disappointments tempt you to get off course.

Persistence is the quality that defies limitations. Persistent people succeed by refusing to accept self-imposed, internal limitations. They are quick to recognize and replace the self-defeating attitudes reflected in the following statements:

- I can't.

- I'm not smart enough.

- I'm afraid to fail.

- Other people deserve to succeed more than I do.

They also reject any perceived external limitations, such as the following:

- Women are not welcome in my company's boardroom.

- Others will thwart my success because my ideas are unconventional.

- My supervisors will discount my technical abilities because of my physical disability.

Make a determination to stick with your vision and life's purpose and do the things that serve your desired outcomes. If you do, you will reach your destination and make a valuable contribution—to your family, your community, and your world. In turn, your contribution to others will reward and strengthen you by causing your vision to become even more alive in your heart.

Edison's contributions to society fueled his passion; therefore, he continued to be productive long after the achievement of his first invention. Long before he died, Edison had revolutionized his world and laid the foundation for the great technological advances of the twentieth and twenty-first centuries!

LIVING "LARGE": THE RIGHT RESULTS FOR THE RIGHT REASONS

At its core, this book's purpose is to encourage and support you in being the "biggest you" possible. That means fulfilling your potential and enjoying your life without the hindrances and poor results generated by misbeliefs, misunderstandings of self-worth, or misrepresentations of the person you were created to be.

There was only one Thomas Alva Edison, but your potential for destiny is just as significant as his. However, if you do not believe that you have worth, value, and purpose, you will see yourself as separated by a wide gulf from Thomas Edison and the other *Haves* of the world. And if you relegate yourself to *Have-Not* status, you will live small by default. You will not be able to cooperate with your unique destiny because you won't believe you really have one. If you won't support and validate your life's purpose, who will?

This is precisely where the roots of shame and mistaken identity take their greatest toll: as long as we remain chained to an inaccurate, inappropriate, or destructive self-image, we will exclude ourselves from becoming our biggest selves, and we will continue in the stifling confinement of the old, dysfunctional hiding place.

In that limited environment, you can live, but only as a shadow of your authentic self. Your outcomes will be defined not by your unlimited potential but by what you believe you cannot do or be. The life I just described is lived in grayscale; aspirations and achievements are minimized by the attitude that says, "*Things happen.*" Options are reduced to bare minimum by the inner voice that says, *This is all that I have to choose from.*

Neither you nor I were created to cower in dank, dingy prison cells of our own making. By nature, we want to live in the wide-open spaces and broad horizons inhabited by those who live with gusto and enjoy life fully. And thankfully, we *can* be our biggest selves—but *how*?

In my experience, the way you leave your hiding place behind and rise above the limitations of the past is by developing a vision for your future that is *bigger* than what you used to believe was possible. Once you have such a vision in place, you'll want to cooperate with your vision by cleaving to your life's purpose, checking your motives along the way, and being intentional about your choices and actions.

None of this happens by accident or in the absence of resistance. To go from *having a dream* to *living your dream* requires focus. Staying committed and pushing forward day by day means directing your best energies not toward distractions and time-wasters but toward your stated goals. That means refusing to squander your vitality on old fears or plots to maintain misrepresented or mistaken identities.

It all comes down to your C.A.R.—choice, action, and results. These steps are not a quick fix or fad formula. They are part of an ongoing, lifelong process designed to release you from the hiding place and keep you free.

Every day, you are free to choose whether you will submit to the old voices in your head that said you weren't worthy or good enough. You are free to stop, rewind, and re-record the tape that plays on the big screen of your mind.

You get to choose whether to stick with the status quo or move forward. You have the freedom to act in ways that are consistent with what you really want out of life. You are empowered to evaluate your results and make course corrections as you see fit. You can live really large, but in the end, only the results that are driven by your heartfelt sense of purpose will yield the sweet and lasting fruit you desire.

There was a time in my life when I worked very hard to achieve impressive results, but they left me feeling hollow and unsatisfied. When I stood to my feet after being thrown in the greasy gutter that awful night so many years ago, I decided to turn my life around...and I did. I knew where I had been, and I knew that it was no longer working for me. I had to formulate a way out.

I made a lifestyle switch and learned to focus my strengths, energy, and talents to achieve specific goals. I disciplined myself to the point that I was able to perform at the level required to become a world record-holder and a world-cup champion.

I left my hiding place and the passivity it demanded so that I could take charge of my life and make the most of my talents, strength, and time. I performed physical feats very well and rose to the top of my sport, but when I stood before people as a champion, I was still emotionally wounded. That woundedness drove me to achieve good things for less than the best reasons.

I was physically strong, and as far as others could tell, I was strong on the inside, too. The truth was that my emotional growth had been seriously stunted. This became evident to me through the incident I described in Chapter 6 when I became despondent over the words used to describe my breaking of the world record.

Moments before despair enveloped me, I was sitting on top of the world. What I did not realize until later was that my elation was due mostly to the fact that my accomplishment made me feel better about myself. I needed to perform and achieve victory far too desperately. My excellent goals were reached for the wrong reasons or for reasons that weren't completely sound.

The debacle brought me to the realization that my course was in need of another correction. Without such an adjustment, I would have turned my profession into another, shinier, higher-stakes hiding place, and each victory would have been one more polished shield behind which I could hide my brokenness.

In time and with careful attention to my motives, my responses to others, and my own emotions, I began to focus my energies on more productive activities and healthier goals. Little by little, I discovered how to cooperate with a big vision for my life—one that was big for the right reasons.

CREATE THE BOUNCE

Consider five choices you have made, actions you have taken, or detriments you have tolerated that may be draining the energy you need to live large according to our explanation of becoming your biggest self. Write them down in the spaces provided.

1. _____

_____

2. _____

_____

3. _____

_____

4. _____

_____

5. _____

_____

Now consider five course corrections you can make so that your best energy can be better harnessed and focused on productive activities and improved outcomes. List the adjustments you plan to make in the spaces provided.

1. _____

_____

2. _____

_____

3. _____

_____

4. _____

_____

5. _____

_____

Practice seeing your results (including your grandest accomplishments and most haunting disappointments) as being part of a well-rounded life. Handle your outcomes with respect and tender loving care, because they are key stepping stones to your future. Outcomes of every kind are sharpening tools designed to prepare you for a terrific destiny—the one you, and only you, were created to live!

Chapter 9

TAKE THE EDGE—LAUNCH YOUR BIGGEST LIFE!

"And the day came when the risk to remain tight in a bud was more painful than the risk it took to blossom."[1]

—Anais Nin

WHEREVER you are at this moment in your life, whatever choices are past, whatever results you have experienced, whatever unexplained occurrences have become part of your life story, you are perched on the pivot point I call *the edge*.

Taken individually and in combination, the qualities of your edge are unique. The confluence of circumstances and opportunities you face are unmatched in your prior experience and in the experiences of others. Although every edge has certain fundamental markers, the "now" edge in your life is like no other.

We are not talking here about stunt work experiences on the soaring upper edge of an eighty-story building. Yet, the options all of us face in life's edge moments are strikingly similar to those I discovered hundreds of feet above terra firma:

You can stand frozen on the edge and pretend to be comfortable there.

Or you can use the edge as your launch pad to your destiny.

To teeter on the edge without crossing over requires a great deal of energy and maintenance of the status quo. To launch out from the edge requires the taking of ownership and the making of decisions about the life you choose to live. In the first case, you will use your strength and power to stand still. In the second, your vitality will be dedicated to forward motion.

Either way, a measure of risk is involved. If you stay on this side of the edge, the possibility of an unintentional fall remains. If you decide to take the edge and launch into a bigger life, you risk the discomfort of dealing with the unknown and the mistakes explorers inevitably make when advancing into new territory.

With each set of risks there are also rewards. Though the cost of launching may seem exorbitant to those of us who have been in hiding for any length of time, the costs of passivity are higher still. As John F. Kennedy put it, "There are risks and costs to a program of action. But they are far less than the long-range risks and costs of comfortable inaction."[2]

You didn't read this far because you were ready to settle for the status quo. Chances are you are restless on the edge and finding it increasingly difficult to remain frozen and feign comfort there. On the backside of the edge is an imperfect past that is not subject to improvement. However, beyond the edge is the opportunity to discover your authentic life—an overcoming life.

The past is what it is, or rather what it was. The future—now that's another story.

READY TO REDESIGN YOUR LIFE?

Go ahead—gasp. The question is provocative; it brings each of us toes up and nose to nose with the real and perceived barriers we have slammed into before. When we tried hard and failed to hurtle over them, discouragement and a wounded self-image convinced many of us to straddle them instead.

Over time, your dreams and goals of reaching the other side of the edge can slip away. That does not mean they have expired; you *can* get back in the game. Your life remains yours to design, and you can redesign it until what you have is working for you. It's a matter of putting your choices and actions to work in order to bring about your *desired* results.

Redesign my life? I'm not sure I can handle the one I've got! That's precisely the point—to create a life you can enjoy. Life is, by nature, a series of adjustments, and no one can make them for us. We can let life wash over us, or we can *do* something. And yes, it takes focus and an ownership mentality. But as human beings we have:

- The freedom to choose

- The responsibility to act

- Accountability for our results.

This is your *life*. Only you can choose what kind of life it will be and what kind of impact it will have. And guess what? You are already light years beyond your hiding place, even if nothing but your thinking has changed up to this point.

Yes—you have come this far! The genie is out of the bottle, and stuffing her back in really isn't worth the trouble. You've got bigger fish to fry and much more life ahead. So let's take what we have discovered about *choice, action, and results* and apply it to develop the lives we really want to live.

We can begin with three key life redesign steps that will start the launch clock running. Welcome to your opportunity to redefine boundaries, reframe internal structures, and imagine the life you were created to live!

BOUNDARIES DEFINE IDENTITY

Emotionally and relationally speaking, *boundaries* are the membranes delineating the space each of us occupies in relation to one another. Boundaries clarify individual identity and responsibility. They also regulate what enters our individual space and help us to assess whether that content is beneficial or detrimental, appropriate or inappropriate.

Redefine boundaries. Do you remember our Chapter 6 discussion about *choosing to redefine* self? We considered the comedy act of Rodney Dangerfield and his "I don't get no respect" persona. We explored the power of choice and its application to the establishment of authentic identity.

The point was that, unless the Dangerfield character was willing to let go of his sad-sack persona and victim mentality, he could not properly honor and respect himself, and he certainly could not command the respect of others.

Redefining ourselves is a legitimate way to shed inauthentic, self-sabotaging identities. An important part of the redefinition process is the setting or resetting of boundaries that define and preserve identity.

Not all boundaries are healthy. You'll remember how I, as a child, inadvertently crossed unspoken boundaries established by others. I was a vibrant, effusive youngster and hadn't learned to fit into the box others defined for me.

Because I learned to tolerate the inappropriate conduct of others, my healthy boundaries began to erode. Worse, because I perceived that others misused their strength to overstep boundaries, I moved past the point of passivity and used my emotional strength to resist the formation and maintenance of healthy boundaries. These boundaries would have conveyed the following essential messages to others:

- I know where I begin and end.

- I have identity definition and a unique place in this world.

- I honor and respect who I am.

Instead, the absence of boundaries conveyed my lack of self-definition and telegraphed my proclivity to remain inappropriately vulnerable. This contributed to the formation and entrenchment of the inauthentic identity of emotional *ragdoll*.

The establishment of sound boundaries would have directed my interaction more constructively and would have helped me to evaluate my own behavior more accurately. With a clearer sense of identity and conduct, I would have experienced improved relational outcomes and increased self-confidence.

This is part of the value of healthy boundaries. They define identity and create accountability. With boundaries firmly in place, we can hold ourselves and others to appropriate standards. In this healthy environment, we can function regardless of our imperfections and the flaws of others. We can make peace with the reality that we are all imperfect; therefore, we can release ourselves from compulsive and damaging perfectionism.

Whether you already have healthy boundaries in place or are contending with boundary erosion, you remain empowered to choose. You are free to define *and* redefine boundaries at any time until they work for you and promote mutually beneficial interaction. You are *always* at choice.

Reframe your internal structure. In Chapter 3, I invited you to reframe your thought life by replacing any damaging self-talk with new thoughts based in the reality of your intrinsic value as a human being.

Healthy boundaries will help support the installment of this positive self-talk. Boundaries also support your internal structure—the person you are on the inside. Your internal structure includes your beliefs, attitudes, thoughts, habits, intellect, feelings, and identity. This internal structure is the framework of your life; it is what upholds you and guides your choices and actions.

To redesign your life, you will want to examine your framework and reframe it where needed. You have already discovered and undertaken some areas of reframing. You've discovered how to:

- Identify your hiding place

- Check your gait

- Take ownership of your thought life

- Detect your invisible wheelchair

- Value your authentic identity...and more.

Our purpose here is to provide a template for the reframing process—one you can use in the context of your life's vision and purpose. This template will serve as a resource for your continued pursuit of ever-higher levels of freedom, bearing in mind that life is an ongoing process of transformation and growth opportunities always exist.

When it comes to redesigning your life, two fundamental elements are necessary for the process of reframing to be fully successful:

1. A vision-based blueprint to guide the reframing process.

2. The clearing of space for the reframe to be undertaken.

Consider these requirements in relation to the physical process of reframing a home. The builder begins with a concept; a blueprint is created; the reframing is completed according to the specifications of the blueprint.

The process of *life-reframing* works much the same way. You start with a vision for your life and from that vision you create a blueprint. In Chapter 8, we explored the topic of vision and established the following statements about the qualities and implications of having a vision for your life:

- A compelling vision determines your course.

- Your vision is worthy of being articulated.

- Your vision is linked to your purpose.

- Your purpose and your vision will measure your results.

- Vision illuminates your values, and values govern your approach to achievement.

- Vision supports attitudes and behaviors that enhance your results.

Your vision is the foundation of your reframe, just as your life purpose is the foundation of your vision. To achieve your intended redesign, develop a clear picture in your own mind of what you were created to achieve and what you want out of life.

You are not a ragdoll designed to end up anywhere in life that you happen to land. You are a strong person who is taking ownership of his or her results. You have preferences, and you have power. With your preferences in mind and your power in play, you can influence your life outcomes in extraordinary ways!

Let's return to our real-life reframe parallel for a moment. We know that, before the reframing of a physical structure can begin, there must first be a demolition process. Before demolition gets underway, there must be enough space cleared for the work to take place.

This gutting begins with the removal of whatever stuff is inside. Furniture, curtains, personal belongings—everything—must be hauled away. Once the structure is bare, the building features that are no longer useful must be demolished.

Walls, partitions, and hallways that once guided the occupants through the internal spaces of the structure are brought down in order to create what a designer would call a better flow.

Some of the doors that served to divide the spaces must be removed so that the desired design can be achieved. Old, weathered windowpanes and clogged screens that have hung in place for years must come down. Once they are removed, the occupants realize just how obstructed and diminished their perspective had become.

Emotionally speaking, a space in the process of reframing is cleared of old internal structures that will be unsuitable in the newly defined space. These include misbeliefs, mistaken identities, misplaced fears, and distortions of self-image. This clearing out of what has become obsolete produces increased clarity; it improves outlook and supports the pursuit of our dreams. And because it is based on a vision-based blueprint, it will produce the results you intended.

Know what you want, and put your imagination to work. Ultimately, your reframe is only as good as the desire and vision that drive it. Likewise, desire and vision are defined by the extent to which you are able or will allow yourself to picture what you want.

In every life endeavor, what matters most is not what others say but what you *believe*. Feelings, behaviors, and outcomes rise and fall on the strength and quality of our beliefs. Belief is your internal motivator, the most powerful change-maker, and the most reliable provider of life-transforming know-how.

This is the reason we focused so intently on identifying and uprooting mis-beliefs. Belief drives action; therefore, until what you believe is compatible with what you want in life, you cannot experience a fundamental, transformative, and lasting change for the better.

Belief is the internal drive designed to sustain and undergird your forward motion until the person you are becoming is fully evident. In other words, your beliefs will keep you afloat while you navigate the tricky waters of transition; they will support your dream when no other proof of your dream is yet available.

When people ask how my life changed so dramatically, I answer without hesitation by saying, "The changes you see on the outside began with change of heart." My beliefs changed in several key ways:

- I decided that freedom was my God-given right.

- I believed that freedom was attainable.

- I imagined what a life of freedom would be like.

Once my heart changed, everything else began to fall into place. It was a domino effect that started with one gentle push. Had the change within me not occurred, I would still be that storm-tossed ragdoll ceding my personal power to anyone and anything that pressured me to do so.

But the key had turned, and the starkness of my reality hit me: I had lived as a ragdoll too long. My unwarranted submission to external forces had taken a toll and left me with a severely compromised identity. I was not willing to live that way any longer.

Anyone who has been hiding to any degree—in any area of life—for any length of time arrives at a similar crossroads. You realize that your existing life design is *not working* for you, and you become aware of the desperate need for a do-over. In your mind's eye you catch a fleeting glimpse a new life design, one that is based on new, more grounded belief system.

That is your point of decision, the place at which the edge becomes your launch pad into an authentic, fulfilling, purposeful life. To power the launch, you will need to use your God-given imagination to envision life on the other side of the edge.

Your ability to imagine this new life will cause the old walls that once trapped you to disintegrate as though they had been hit by a wrecking ball. No longer will emotional barriers keep you imprisoned; no longer will they speak convincingly to say: *What you want is impossible; you can't get there from here.*

You absolutely *can* get there from here. You were created to get there from here. You were meant to be filled with life and by life. Conversely, you were designed to be uncomfortable with a sense of emptiness. That's why humans relentlessly seek to fill the empty places! The two-fold question becomes:

1. In what healthy ways can that emptiness to be filled?

2. What would a full life look like?

Even when unmet needs are masked over, they are always demonstrated. Their existence is exposed by the behaviors they drive at the unconscious level. These behaviors are most often negative or self-sabotaging. Therefore, the importance of knowing what you want and need cannot be overstated.

Make time and space to imagine the breadth of the life you desire. Live large in your thoughts so that you can live large in reality. Accept the *you* that now is, so you can embrace the *you* that is in the process of becoming.

Accept whatever state of wholeness is evident in your being at this moment, knowing that your overall condition is not static, but subject to change. You are becoming more whole with every step you take away from your former hiding place.

Most importantly, refuse to condemn or stand in judgment of your in-process self. (Remember that *life is a process*.) When you disapprove rather than encourage yourself, you invite judgment to shut down your life and prohibit yourself the necessary room to grow, change, and thrive.

RISK WHAT ISN'T WORKING FOR WHAT WILL

Every *at-choice* moment reminds us that our decisions (including the decision not to choose) open the door to risk and reward.

We have explored risks of various kinds. In Chapter 1, I shared with you how my need for approval had cost me a life of emotional exile. Leaving that awful but strangely comfortable environment opened me up to the risk of further rejection and the experience of discomfort in unfamiliar surroundings.

Yet, those risks have proven worth taking; the rewards of freedom are much greater than whatever losses I might have suffered. My life today is so much richer, more colorful, and infinitely more fulfilling. The range of my life experiences has been greatly expanded, and the opportunities I encounter are far greater in number and quality than ever before. Not only that, but it is evident to me that my experiences are tied to my purpose and destiny. Therefore, my life is more meaningful and satisfying to me and brings more benefit to others.

Still, the issue of risk remains and warrants further exploration. So far, we have touched upon several kinds of risk over the course of this book. In no particular order of importance, they include some variation of the following risks:

- Leaving the familiarity of the past behind and taking ownership of the present

- Choosing to be transparent and authentic rather than hiding behind mistaken identities

- Becoming more spontaneous and therefore more vulnerable

- Opting for freedom by making unfamiliar decisions and taking unproven actions

- Choosing to act in a manner consistent with purpose-driven goals, even if you see yourself as a *Have Not.*

There *are* risks involved with regaining freedom. However, there are even greater risks to be faced in captivity. To remain in hiding requires that we find endless ways to cope with the pain involved.

Many numb themselves to the pain because experiencing it would be intolerable and would call into question valuable relationships and protected belief systems. Some repress or postpone the effects of pain, compartmentalizing them so as to continue their lives without emotional disruption. Some mask the effects of pain with mistaken identities or with addictive behaviors.

When we fail to acknowledge and deal with pain in order to remain in a familiar hiding place, we do so at a price. The costs vary for everyone, but among the charges exacted are the following:

- Deeper entrenchment in old paradigms, self-sabotaging belief systems, and counterproductive patterns of behavior, leading to impaired outcomes

- Emotional and relational inaccessibility and therefore exclusion from relational intimacy and fulfillment

- Passivity prompted by the fear of negative outcomes and therefore self-prohibition from forward progress

- Feelings of inferiority that undermine goal-setting and prevent fulfillment of purpose.

Whatever your fears or misgivings (whether well-placed or generated by misbeliefs), always be willing to clearly assess the balance of risk and reward in relation to life's growth opportunities. Doing so will help you to override misplaced fears and reap the rewards you truly desire.

CREATE THE BOUNCE

Assess both where you are in your life journey and who you are at this precise moment. Without condemning or levying judgment, consider how taking the risks listed below (whether for the first time or in increasing measure, whichever applies) would help to produce the following three rewards:

1. A more productive life and increased benefit to others, immediately and in the longer term.

2. An improved personal life, in terms of interaction with others, career advancement, and improved emotional and physical health.

3. A transformed belief system in regard to your potential, effectiveness, and unique abilities.

Note: Please answer in specific terms. For instance, in describing aspects of improved emotional and physical health in relation to leaving the past behind, avoid over-generalized statements such as *I would be happier.* Instead, formulate your answer more along these lines:

Leaving the past behind would help me to be more engaged and optimistic regarding the circumstances of my life and would enable me to look forward to, rather than dread, tomorrow.

These specifics will help you to discern where you are and precisely what you stand to gain by taking the well-founded risks associated with becoming your biggest self.

Answer Questions 1-3 in Regard to the Following Risks:

- Leaving the familiarity of the past behind and taking ownership of an opportunity in the present

- Choosing to be transparent and authentic with loved ones rather than hiding behind mistaken identities

- Becoming more spontaneous in response to circumstances and relationships, and therefore more vulnerable

- Opting for freedom in a particular situation by making unfamiliar decisions and taking unproven actions

- Choosing to act in a manner consistent with purpose-driven goals, even if you see yourself as a Have Not.

The Rewards to be Gained:

Some people claim to be born risk-takers. That may be so, but in my experience we learn best by doing. By taking reasonable, well-considered risks, we gain experience in making decisions. We begin to realize that risk-taking is part of life, and we learn to take occasional failures in stride. Over time, we gain confidence in our ability to take the right risks for the right reasons. As a result, we achieve more satisfying outcomes and become more productive overall.

LAUNCH INTO AN *OVERCOMING* LIFE

When you walk away from the hiding place, healing and recovery are already underway. From your moment of decision, the point at which you choose to pursue freedom and authenticity, the paradigms once erected for self-protection become bothersome. They look old. They seem heavier than before. Their stale, musty scent is conspicuous and unappealing.

When you seize the pivotal moments in life—when you take ownership of the edge and transform it into your launch pad—you will leave the baggage of the hiding place behind. The camouflage, defenses, masks, and other barriers that served their critical purpose in the jungle are not needed in the open terrain of freedom.

This exit from hiding is part of the recovery process in which you regain what had been surrendered, including your authentic identity and the life you were created to live.

Recovery is a worthy goal. With that first step out of the emotional underworld and into real living, we recover the realization that we are not required to live through others, or hold our breath until they breathe first, or wait for permission to speak or create. We accept the invitation to make our own moves and see the world through our own eyes. We begin to take ownership of the life each of us has been given by making choices that serve our individual purposes and meet our unique needs. We decide who we are and who we are becoming, without seeking permission or approval from others. This gradual return to wholeness cannot happen in hiding; it can only happen out in the open.

Consider the process of recovery from a physical setback. If you've ever suffered a disabling injury, had a surgery, or gone through chemotherapy, you probably remember the longing to regain your strength. You know how good it felt to get back on your feet and return to "normal" life.

When in the midst of crises like these, your turnaround begins with the desire to reclaim your physical "ground zero"—the level playing field where your life used to unfold with everyone else's. You envision yourself doing simple errands and everyday chores. You imagine driving the kids to school and emptying the dishwasher! Your initial goal is to get back to where you were before your life was interrupted.

Emotional healing is a parallel process. When you catch your first glimpse of the place called *freedom*, you become eager to get there. Compared to your hiding place, this emotional ground zero looks inviting. In fact, it looks so good that you might want to build a monument and camp out there. Yet, when you take your first taste of authentic living, the question quickly becomes: *Is recovery my end goal, or can I take the edge completely and live as an overcomer?*

A look at recent American history speaks to the idea of *overcoming*. During one of the most tumultuous periods in the United States, as Americans grappled with the issues of race and equality, Dr. Martin Luther King, Jr., spoke powerfully of the power of people to overcome.

Dr. King fought tirelessly for the rights of African Americans. He did this in very practical ways designed to bring societal change and eliminate discriminatory practices. He longed for the day when all Americans lived and worked on a level playing field—the day when the civil and human rights of every man, woman, and child were honored, not only in word, but also in deed.

Dr. King also addressed the issue of an individual's personal power. He knew that lasting change would come only when the internal barriers within all people were confronted. These emotional barriers included bigotry, fear, and diminished self-worth.

Dr. King knew that hatred had to be dealt with and so did shame. The day would have to come when African Americans would be treated fairly under the law. But he also understood that, because external forms of oppression had left painful internal scars, civil rights reform would not be enough.

The following quotes from Dr. King describe the dual challenges of discrimination and the emotional bruises caused by centuries of injustice:

Discrimination is a hellhound that gnaws at Negroes in every waking moment of their lives to remind them that the lie of their inferiority is accepted as truth in the society dominating them.[3]

Change does not roll in on the wheels of inevitability, but comes through continuous struggle. And so we must straighten our backs and work for our freedom. A man can't ride you unless your back is bent.[4]

Externally, discrimination had disadvantaged an entire race, but Dr. King understood that unless the individual identities of the disadvantaged were restored to wholeness, oppression would continue to hold court in their hearts. Although human and civil rights might be *recovered*, the effects of discrimination would not be *overcome*.

Recovery is a process based in external motivators. We can see this from examples in the recovery movement, such as twelve-step programs. Millions have recovered from addictions and other detrimental behaviors and relationships through programs of this kind.

In the twelve-step process, participants join support groups, adhere to accountability practices, and take part in other externally-driven activities designed to keep them free from the offending habit.

According to the prevailing philosophy in many programs, participants can never be free of their addictions; instead they are suspended in the perpetual act of *recovering*. For example, in alcohol-related programs of this kind, participants accept this important concept: Even if they quit drinking for the remainder of their lives, they will forever retain the title of *alcoholic*.

It is important to understand that, while drinking is a behavior, being an alcoholic is an identity. While I am thankful for the successes achieved and the lives saved in recovery programs, I believe there is a "thirteenth step" beyond recovery. That step is *to overcome*.

Overcoming occurs when the fruit of recovery takes an internal position in one's identity. Instead of "right" behaviors resulting from external suggestions or prohibitions, they result from self-permission to make good choices. In other words, choice based in belief becomes the motivation that anchors the person to beneficial behaviors.

For the sake of example, we'll assume that someone named Melissa had a history of co-dependency. Melissa knew she couldn't get free of her emotional addiction without a support system, so she joined a support group. The rules and activities observed by the group helped Melissa to understand the dangers of co-dependency and helped her to resist co-dependent behaviors and relationships. We would say Melissa was recovering from her addiction.

To *overcome* in the area of co-dependency, Melissa would eventually move beyond the place where external supports and constraints would impel her to override her co-dependent tendencies. Instead, Melissa would arrive at a place where her authentic identity was healed and in command.

At that point, Melissa's co-dependent behaviors would be organically replaced with the behaviors generated by her authentic identity as a non-codependent woman. Melissa's re-seated healthy needs and wants would have rendered co-dependency unnecessary and unappealing.

Granted, this takes time. External constraints are a perfectly legitimate means to a desired end. Yet, I firmly believe that recovery is not a final destination; instead, it is a step in the process of overcoming. It is when a mistaken identity is finally cast off that we can become truly free of the detrimental behaviors that were attached to it. Then, the authentic identity will empower us to live the overcoming life of freedom that is the true goal.

IT'S ALWAYS SPRINGTIME

To paraphrase Anais Nin, *the risk to remain tight in a bud is more painful than the risk it will take to blossom.* Whatever the season, your springtime begins every time you awaken to a new morning. Every day is another opportunity to blossom!

You are an amazing individual, and you are standing on the edge of *something*. (Everyone is!) Your edge is yours to take, and you are invited to *take it* and use it as a launch pad into a bigger, better, more fulfilling life—the powerfully overcoming life you were born to live.

Chapter 10

EXPERIENCE TRANSFORMATION: FROM INVISIBLE TO TRANSPARENT

"Beauty is truth, truth beauty—that is all Ye know on Earth, and all ye need to know."
—John Keats,
"Ode on a Grecian Urn"

TRUTH *is* beautiful. And while we fondly say that beauty is in the eye of the beholder, we know that truth does not bend its knee to a point of view. Truth just *is*. Transparent yet visible, truth is welcoming and unafraid. It commands respect and never wavers.

Your authentic identity is truth-based. There is no one more beautiful than the person you were created to be. Accessible, transparent, and genuine in every detail, the person you are inside is strong, shameless, and resilient.

Some may feel threatened by the authentic you; it may be that they are not yet comfortable in their own skins. Still, your authentic identity will draw to you those who value the genuine and prize the precious. You will never be more free than to reveal the real you to the world!

You know my story. I grew up feeling like I was too much and not enough all at the same time. So I hid my authentic identity under layers of self-protection and preservation that were so heavy I could barely breathe under the weight of them. I believed that others forced me to become invisible; yet, I embraced the emotional safety of my invisibility and labored with every heartbeat to remain cloaked in it.

Still, there was a bright spot in my early life, one sunny place where I could catch my breath and be myself—in the company of my grandmother. I had never known anyone like Nana; no one seemed to love me as she did. Nana's face would light up whenever I came into the room. She always had time to greet me, hug me, converse with me. She took pleasure in being good to me and loved to cut my cantaloupe just the way I liked it.

Nana saw me much differently than I saw myself. To her, I was valuable, a bundle of joy, worthy of being indulged and loved. Nana *saw* me; she saw the *real* me. She believed in the person I was and the person I was becoming. She told me I could be anything I wanted to be.

Nana understood me, and in the rare moments when she didn't, she affirmed and accepted me. She gave her attention freely, and I absorbed her lovingkindness into my very being as nourishment to my starving soul. When I was with Nana, I could be myself and feel good about it. I was neither invisible nor a ragdoll; I was Nana's "Terri doll."

What Does *Invisible* Look Like?

The question, *"What does Invisible look like?"* seems paradoxical. After all, *invisible* doesn't look like anything at all; invisible can't be seen. Yet there is more to invisibility than a simple disappearing act. Consider the following *Random House* definitions of *invisible*:

- Not visible; not perceptible by the eye

- Withdrawn from or out of sight; hidden

- Not perceptible or discernible by the mind[2]

Allow me to share the kind of *invisible* with which I am familiar, the kind that is "withdrawn from or out of sight," or "hidden." The kind that, technically speaking, can be seen, but is never noticed. A memory from my childhood conveys the sense of this aspect of invisibility.

I remember a certain house that our family used to live in. It had an attic that was stuffy and dark, covered over in years of disregard and imposed obscurity.

Our attic was not a place where treasures were kept; it was what I call the *throw-away room*, the place where unwanted things were not so much stored, as tossed...out of sight and out of mind.

In this room for forgotten things, I remember seeing a ragdoll partially crushed under the sharp edge of a heavy box. She had obviously been pinned there for years, half of her limp body covered and half exposed.

The exposed part revealed her dreadful state: the thread that held her together was coming undone; her stuffing was escaping through her unraveling seams; and her hair was disheveled, matted in years of dust, grime, and darkness.

As I leaned over to free her broken body from the heaviness she had borne so long, I saw myself in her—a ragdoll overlooked, uncared for, devalued, dismembered, and cast aside. She, too, was visible, yet had gone unnoticed, carelessly stepped on by those who were preoccupied with more important matters.

Like all of us, she had been created to belong and to bring joy to others. Yet, she had been set aside, disconnected, and concealed in a hidden place where she could exist in obscurity, never intruding upon their lives or territory.

Hers was the kind of invisibility with which I could identify. I imagined that, if she were alive, she would have desired release from the heavy edge entrapping her. Yet she lay motionless and, like me, silently awaited a rescue that might never come.

I identified deeply with the ragdoll in the throw-away room. Although our respective hiding places are dark and unappealing, they were quiet and familiar. I seemed to fit better in my hiding place than I did anywhere else. And if I couldn't find my place in the world or my family, I could carve out a place for myself where no one else wanted to be.

I learned that it was much easier to be hidden than to be misunderstood. It was easier to go unseen than unaccepted. It was easier to voluntarily disconnect from my dreams than to have them ripped from my heart. So I created a shroud of coping behaviors that rendered me invisible and buried my pain along with my identity.

In hiding, I found the way to avoid rejection and to glean the morsels of approval that could be won through misplaced tolerance. I reformulated my relationships so that others would learn to treat me the way I saw myself:

- Unwanted

- Beneath others

- Unworthy

- Used and abused

- Overlooked

- Belonging nowhere

- Undeserving of respect.

I call this kind of overdone self-protection *padding in*. Whether it is done consciously or not, it is the careful arranging of one's life to shut down the pain centers and shut out the surrounding world. Since I saw transparency as the ultimate exposure to danger, I used my strength to become opaque and imperceptible. I kept everyone at whatever emotional distance made me feel safe and performed flawlessly at a level I hoped would indemnify me against criticism.

All I really managed to accomplish was a complete disconnect from my own heart. I had tried to remain invisible by becoming completely imperceptible. I failed to understand the repercussions: No one was allowed to see beneath the outermost layer of my skin, not even me.

I had successfully encased myself in a throw-away room built one wall at a time. It began with the creation of a purely emotional shell, but over time, the shell took other forms. High school provided an identity based on structure and activity. But when I graduated, I had no internal structure to hold me together, and I descended into a life of drug abuse and co-dependency.

Much later, my titles of *athlete* and *stuntperson* provided bright, shiny shields behind which I could hide. The coolness and toughness of these roles enabled me to direct the attention of others to my spectacular *doing* rather than my fractured *being*. This was my way of keeping the disapproved part of me invisible while keeping everyone's eyes fixed on my strength, accomplishments, and trophies.

But inside, I was still a ragdoll dependent upon the approval of others. Gold medals, notoriety, the ability to look bigger on the outside than I felt on the inside—none of these artifices were able to end my suffering. They were constructed for the wrong reasons and yielded the wrong results. I achieved the recognition I craved, but it only made me less transparent.

That's what being *invisible* looked like to me.

ENTER THE LAND OF THE SUPERHEROES

Invisibility based on performance can take on many forms, individually and on societal levels.

The modern Western woman knows something about performance mentality. On the positive side, she has gained entrance into circles that were once closed to her. She been released from many stereotypes of generations past and has more choices available to her than ever before.

However, the shiny shield of liberation is heavy and demands a high level of performance. Too often, it requires a super-heroic effort and a bullet-proof identity. Overachievement becomes the standard that must be maintained in order to attain some semblance of success as woman, wife, mother, provider, or professional.

To keep all the plates spinning at once, she must summon every ounce of her energy and exploit any reserves. This is especially true for those who are driven from within to perform perfectly on all fronts. This high-performance individual all too easily becomes a rotating human hat-rack—a roulette wheel of identities to be mastered and marveled at, a superhero who never sleeps.

That is not to say that every woman who achieves at a high level is hiding under the "hats" she wears. Many women are living the lives of their dreams; they have found ways to make it work and have managed to maintain a healthy sense of self. But for many, over-achievement is a way to gain approval and a longed-for sense of acceptance. For those who are teetering under the weight of it all, the superhero mask eventually cracks.

Superhero does not always equal *bad*, however. In fact, there's one superhero from whom I have learned something. She is the only superhero I know who works wonders without hiding. Her unmasked persona gives me some insight into the value of truth and transparency. Her name is *Wonder Woman.*

Wonder Woman was created in 1941 by William Marston, a Harvard-trained psychologist known for his work in developing the lie detector. Moonlighting under the pseudonym Charles Moulton, Marston created the premier female comic book hero, a displaced princess from the Amazon who worked with the Allies to defeat the Axis powers.

Wonder Woman reveals a unique blend of attributes; she embraces her strength while moving in a kind of vulnerable grace; she is willing to be known and even romanced. She says what she means, and she means what she says. She is known for her integrity and her pursuit of truth.

Armed with indestructible, bullet-deflecting cuff bracelets and her famous Lasso of Truth, Wonder Woman does more than ward off the bad guys; she forces them to 'fess up. Her unbreakable lasso can restrain characters as powerful as Superman and Captain Marvel and anyone reined in by the lasso cannot help but tell the truth.[3]

Her tiara, symbolic of her grace and femininity, also serves as a weapon that can be thrown to attack an enemy or to defend from a distance. Her sword can split electrons from their atoms, and her plane, which is undetectable by radar or human sight, can vacillate between transparency and a state that renders itself and its occupants invisible to the bad guys.

What I find most fascinating about Wonder Woman is her winning combination of unabashed power and unambiguous nature. She is an unconflicted champion who can wear a tiara *and* perform feats of daring. Her authentic identity is multi-faceted, yet integrated. She is definitively and proudly female, yet comfortable with her strength and able to command her space. She has strong beliefs about right and wrong and is open about them. She relies as strongly on the power of truth as any other weapon in her arsenal. In fact, truth is at the top of her list of core values.

CROWNED BY STRENGTH AND GRACE

Wonder Woman is no wallflower. In fact, she's the antithesis of one who hides. She's comfortable with her conspicuousness and able to harmonize the wide-ranging nuances of her personality. Wonder Woman is the personification of strength and grace in perfect balance. Her tiara highlights this equilibrium: it is beautiful and graceful, yet powerful. She refuses to wear a mask. Instead, she promotes truth and uses it to make the world a better, safer place.

WHAT DOES *TRANSPARENT* LOOK LIKE?

Before we can answer that question, let's consider this one: Is there a difference between something you *can't see* and something you can *see through*?

You have seen dictionary definitions for the word *invisible*. Now consider some *Random House* definitions of *transparent*:

- So sheer as to permit light to pass through; diaphanous.

- Easily seen through, recognized, or detected

- Manifest; obvious:

- Open; frank; candid.[4]

184

The glaring difference between invisibility and transparency involves detectability. And whether or not we choose to be detected (perceived or discerned) has a lot to do with the way in which we approach the shedding of light upon our authentic identities.

When I choose to be invisible, my goal is to avoid exposure, scrutiny, and the victimization I believe will follow. What I fear is being placed at the mercy of those who will discover the ugly truth about me. From the confines of this mindset, I resist having light shed upon my identity—or more correctly, what I believe to be my identity.

However, when I choose to be transparent, I don't see the shedding of light or the scrutiny of others as being invasive. Because I want to be seen, I cannot be exposed. Instead, I am revealed of my own free will. There are no walls to maintain, because I have brought them down and invited others to know me. I have accepted the risk of trusting others (where appropriate); therefore, I am free to share myself and share in the benefits of relationship.

The choice to be transparent has to begin somewhere, but where? I believe it starts where all healthy attitudes and behaviors start—with self-acceptance and freedom from shame. For me, the epiphany began with the realization that acceptance from others would not be possible until I was willing to accept myself.

This revelation was profound, yet the transformation it would foment was incremental. Little by little, I discovered that I could stand face to face with shame, fear, and discouragement without being overwhelmed by them. Instead, I became increasingly able to look beyond emotions and flaws to the person I was becoming. Gradually, I began to love myself, imperfections and all.

Remember that shame is the root of fear. The shame face had been my identity for many years. It was what drove me into hiding and what kept me there so long. When I was finally able to remove the mask of shame, it was like having a facelift: all the years of emotional wear and tear were being undone. The unsound parts of my internal structure were torn down and reframed, and new words and beliefs were building me back up. The mistaken identities my shame demanded could be sloughed off. I remember thinking, *How strangely contradictory this is—as though I could become a superhero, not by putting a mask on, but by taking it off!*

No longer did I need to be seen as impenetrable. I realized for the first time that to be vulnerable and able to admit my secret fears was empowering. Suddenly, the emotional numbness to which I was accustomed began to leave, and I was able to *feel* and to *care*. I was able to give myself the gift of approval, acknowledgment, and love.

I could hear the yearnings of my own heart and reconnect with my dreams. As a result, I was able to listen to others and have genuine compassion for them. I could hear more and speak less, because I was no longer striving to prove myself right.

Because I valued myself, I was able to value others. Because I respected myself, I developed greater respect for others. I didn't feel pitted against anyone but ready to give and receive the help that is fundamental to relationship. I developed genuine concern for the people around me. Because I no longer needed to prove myself worthy of approval, this concern was not about wanting to be seen as a good person. It was a matter of being able to share with others what I had already given myself.

Becoming transparent also meant removing the disguise of false humility. Because overlapping layers of unmet needs had driven my belief system (and therefore my attitudes and behaviors), I habitually put others ahead of myself. In my mind, everyone had to matter more than I did, so I shrank myself down to a size smaller than "too big for my britches." The humility was not genuine because being humble means not having to prove yourself one way or the other.

Finally, transparency allows you to be open about your dreams and desires. This candor is not possible in the hiding place. Here's why:

In the hiding place, survival is the sole objective. From the confines of the hiding place, life is necessarily distilled down to the barest essentials. Although you can live in hiding for a lifetime, you never expect to be there forever. Instead, hiders perceive themselves as transients seeking shelter from a passing storm. Under those conditions, dreams become nonessential; they are ill-suited to a survival lifestyle in temporary quarters.

In the hiding place, the expression of your hopes opens the door to having your hopes dashed. When shame drives self-protection, emotional safety is more important than self-expression or the pursuit of destiny. Dreams and any sense of life purpose are shelved until they can be pursued with the assurance that failure and disappointment can be avoided. Unfortunately, life offers no such guarantees. As long as this level of safety is considered prerequisite, dreams will necessarily be sacrificed.

In the hiding place, the pursuit of your dreams will draw attention from others and undermine invisibility. When you are hiding from perceived external threats, the last thing you want to do is to draw a crowd of critical observers. Your primary concern will not be. "Will I fulfill my destiny?" Instead, you will wonder, "What will others say? How they will judge me? How quickly and painfully will they shoot me down?"

When the veil of shame is lifted and invisibility is no longer a priority, you become free to dream again. Instead of feeling too small to inhabit a big life, you are able to accept yourself as a person who is in the process of becoming and progressing en route to a desired destination. You are no longer embarrassed by your aspirations or afraid to push the envelope of your perceived limits.

The transparent woman sees her choices as being hers to make and her responsibility to manage. She's not awaiting rescue, approval, or permission to become a factor in her world. She was created to have an impact, to fully occupy her life and her role, and to follow her dreams—out in the open space she was created to inhabit.

THE REAL SUPERHERO— 10 HALLMARKS OF YOUR BIGGEST SELF

You don't need a Lasso of Truth or bullet-proof cuffs to be a real-life super-hero. The most heroic thing you can do is to flourish to your fullest capacity as the purpose-driven, completely original human being you are. Remember, *you serve no one playing small.*

Becoming your biggest self will release the dynamics necessary to live your biggest life. That is my dream for you—and for me! Allow me to share ten key qualities of those who refuse to hide. I call them *Terri's Top 10 Hallmarks of Your Biggest Self:*

1. Genuine courage—Being empowered and strengthened from within rather than made to feel strong by outward displays of power. Courage is often demonstrated in what we choose not to do.

2. The posture of power—Carrying yourself in such a way as to command respect rather than demand it. The resolution of unmet needs positions us for success by releasing us from neediness.

3. An overcoming approach—Progressing past the point of recovery to the place of overcoming anything that would undermine your destiny. The overcomer respects the lessons of the past but is not bound by history.

4. Security in being and having (rather than in doing and want-ing)—Embracing life and rejecting performance orientation by recognizing that you are a human *being*, not a human *doing*. Self-worth is not earned by humans; it is inherent in their having been created.

5. Willingness to teach others how to treat you—Becoming an agent of change and part of the solution in your relationships. Self-respect is the foundation of mutual respect.

6. Ownership mentality—Occupying your role in life, thereby gen-erating results and fostering transformation. We cannot change or benefit from what we refuse to own.

7. At-choice attitude—Recognizing that, in every circumstance, you can make a difference by making a choice. Appropriate personal power is at the disposal of every adult.

8. A victor's mindset—Realizing that the difference between *victor* and *victim* is found in the letters "I-M." In other words, "U-R" empowered!

9. Transparency in action—Choosing transparency over invisibility and discerning the difference between the two in every circum-stance. To choose transparency is to invite freedom.

10. Championing your dreams—Advocating for the fulfillment of your dreams by taking fear captive and taking action. Your dreams are yours and only yours to live.

CHECK THE GATE

Consider *Terri's Top 10 Hallmarks of Your Biggest Self* as you answer, in writing, the following questions as they relate to each quality:

1. Describe one way in which you have demonstrated the qualities listed—even if it only happened once!

2. Consider one growth opportunity in regard to each of the ten qualities listed. How might you push past any perceived barriers to embrace the quality more fully?

3. Consider your answers to question 2 and describe how growth in these areas might produce specific improvements in your outcomes.

While you're at it, feel free to personalize the list by adding other qualities you believe are important.

FROM INVISIBLE TO TRANSPARENT— 10 KEYS TO YOUR BIGGEST LIFE

The point of transparency is to release you from the prison of invisibility *and* to remove any barriers to your biggest, best, most-fulfilling life.

When we decide that we are finished with cover-ups and hiding places, the thing we begin to desire is our biggest life—the totality of the lives we were created to live. Once you come out of the shadows, you are ready to open the throttle and drive your C.A.R. (choice, action, results) all the way to the finish line that is your destiny.

Following are ten practical steps to make your trip to transparency complete. They are the how-to points distilled from concepts you have discovered over the course of this book, a take-away of strategies you can implement in order to keep your life expansion going strong. Consider them the Lasso of Truth in your quest for personal accountability and big living.

These are not things that you will do once and tuck away for safekeeping; they are lifestyle markers designed to keep you living your biggest life...for the rest of your life!

TERRI'S TOP 10 KEYS TO YOUR BIGGEST LIFE

1. *Recognize and own your choices in all matters at all times.* The goal is always to create a life that works. If you are uncomfortable with any area of life or dissatisfied with results, then something is not working for you. Here's the best news yet—this kind of shortfall is *not* a problem. It is an invitation to create a solution. Begin by pushing the *pause* button; then simply choose again! Remember that no one can legitimately define you or determine the quality of your life. Your life is defined by the choices you make and the choices you don't.

2. *Strengthen your personal foundation.* Your foundation is your internal structure and the quality of life that flows from that structure. Evaluate your life design and determine whether it supports outcomes that meet your expectations. Don't be afraid to find cracks in your foundation; just reframe as needed. (See Chapters 9, 11, and 12.) Eliminate negative influences and other

distractions and recommit, with tenacity and enthusiasm, to a redesign.

3. *Establish a support system that works for you and is compatible with your desired outcomes.* There is a jet stream that flows through your circle of influence and endeavor. Ride it! Choose to participate in events that help you hone your skills and resources and increase your visibility in your desired field. Engage in activities that help you to operate at your optimal level. Choose wisely to ensure that your well-being and overall life purpose are well served.

4. *Face your fears.* Remind yourself often that courage cannot exist in the absence of fear. Courage is resident within you and is always ready to be engaged. Be determined to make apt decisions even in the presence of opposition. Embrace the emotions that accompany fear, remembering that the human body responds to fear and excitement in identical physiological ways. When fear tempts you to surrender, ask yourself this question: *What will this fear cost me, and am I willing to pay that price for the rest of my life?* Until specific fears are confronted, they will continue to intimidate.

5. *Freely develop the picture of the life you desire.* Abandon arbitrarily imposed boundaries and release yourself from any sense of judgment that limits your life design. Envision your biggest life in detail through the power of your imagination. Return to this vision frequently; become familiar with how your biggest life will look so that you will recognize it when it comes.

6. *Empower yourself to say yes to your desired outcomes by identifying three areas to which you must say no.* Uncover any habits, routines, preoccupations, or desires that compromise your life

design. Redirect the energy and resources made available to habits, routines, preoccupations, and desires that support the results you wish to achieve. Realize that not all incompatible involvements are inherently negative, but all of them distract from your purpose.

7. *Determine in advance what your desired outcomes will give you.* Ask yourself what the implications of achieving your desired outcomes will be. In advance, estimate the yield, be aware of who stands to benefit, establish the price you are willing to pay, and become aware of what further opportunities will be created by your desired outcomes. Also decide how your progress toward these outcomes will be measured. This will help you to know when a specific goal has been reached.

8. *Identify your core values.* Core values are the habits of your heart and a functional part of your authentic identity. Your values help to define your boundaries and therefore your conduct. They are also aligned with and supportive of your unique purpose. Core values help you to understand the *why* of your life mission. When you understand your core values, you will become more proactive, because your values will guide your decisions organically.

9. *Examine what you are tolerating.* Over time, we can inadvertently become tolerant of time-wasters and energy-drainers. Often, these tolerations seem to be insignificant; but taken over time and in combination, the costs can mount up substantially and dilute your efforts and results. Become purposeful in identifying these detractors from purpose and shutting them down, realizing that, absent a proactive approach, they can easily go unnoticed.

10. *Own it—all of it.* Be willing to assess where you are in life, and take responsibility for it. Take ownership of your choices and the

outflow of your choices. Own every opportunity—to act, to hold your fear, to be an agent of change. Go beyond *possession* to the place of *ownership* where you are fully engaged and indentified with the machinations of life. This ownership will empower you to impact your world and replicate your overcoming approach in others.

INVISIBLE NO MORE!

Truth *is* beautiful. It is the foundation upon which transparency is built. Transparency—with self and with others—is the calling card of your well-designed, overcoming, fulfilling life. When transparency is your lifestyle, the cold, dark safety of invisibility loses its appeal, and freedom becomes the banner flying over you.

Soak in that for a moment—then turn the page for some hands-on ways to build a solid, lifelong foundation for total freedom in just ten days!

Chapter 11

REFRAME YOUR FOUNDATION IN 10 DYNAMIC DAYS
DAYS 1–5

"Dreams are the feeling I get when I connect who I am with what I do."
—Terri Cadiente

YOU'VE got a wealth of information under your belt and a sharpened sense of identity, purpose, and desire burgeoning inside. What you have at your disposal is the stuff dreams are made of. Now it's time to rev the engines of your biggest life by putting what you know to work for you.

You needn't go it alone, so here's my invitation to you: Let's partner together for ten vibrant days on a life-changing mission—to reframe, create, and re-create where necessary, the solid personal foundation that will support the life of your dreams.

Think that's unbelievable? In our world of rah-rah infomercials, I can understand why. But I'm not selling anything; I'm sharing something real that has changed my own life, and I know this to be true: In ten days, you can lay the solid personal foundation that will undergird your dreams for the rest of your life.

This is not a formula or magic wand; what I'm talking about is a practical, proactive re-positioning of your thoughts, beliefs, and expectations. The potential impact is limitless. This simple process will move you to a whole new place in your internal life, and once the shift happens on the inside, the circumstances on the outside have no choice but to change.

There is a fabulous future waiting—the one you were *born* to live. And you won't have to design the better mousetrap or reinvent the wheel; we'll walk through ten proven steps together, one day at a time. Ten days from now, you will realize that you are sporting a new, empowered approach to an overcoming life.

This is an interactive process, so keep a pen and notebook handy. Make time for the process. Reflect on each day's passage. Use your notebook to capture your thoughts as you read and as you respond to the interactive elements provided along the way. This will serve to cement the progress you make.

In order to make room for the reframe, you'll need to move some old stuff out of the way and silence any self-limiting, self-censoring voices. Allow big thoughts to rise to the surface and find their full expression. Give your imagination the mental space in which to form new pictures of your future. Invest this time in your future; this is how transformation is birthed!

To help you stay focused, afford yourself the privacy and quiet that will keep you undistracted and present to the moment. Set aside the mental chatter that might otherwise commandeer your thoughts. Don't get sidetracked by the phone or extraneous concerns about errands, work, or worries.

Become fully aware of what is going on inside you and ride the wave of transformation with intentionality. Don't be alarmed or bashful about the epiphanies you experience; you are in the process of rediscovering and reclaiming your authentic identity.

Unexpected thoughts and emotions will pop up. Some of these thoughts will be thrilling; some may be disheartening realizations of self-sabotage. All of it is healthy. Don't bring judgment against yourself. Allow the realizations that occur to inform and guide you in making positive adjustments.

Just as some things will come to mind, others will fall away. As some of the lingering weights of the past begin to drop off, you will find yourself standing taller in your posture of power and striding more boldly across the threshold to your dreams.

CLASSIFIED ACTION

In the film industry, it is customary for stunt coordinators to receive a copy of the script for their evaluation. It is their job to create a breakdown of the action that will be staged on set and to *classify* the scenes that will require stunt work. Hence, the term *classified action*.

Following the entries provided for days 1 through 10, you will find an interactive section entitled *Classified Action* in which questions will be provided to help you classify, or break down, your thought processes and actions into manageable pieces.

Be determined to fully exploit this process in order to turn your edge into your launch pad. As you read the passages and engage the interactive elements, pay attention to what is going on internally by taking four key emotional and intellectual readings:

1. *Notice* any fears and fear-based responses.

2. *Assess* any perceived risks; evaluate your risk tolerance.

3. *Choose* your attitude; assume the posture of power.

4. Take *action* that is aligned with your desired outcomes.

In each section, make a conscious effort to be transparent, completely visible, and accepting of yourself. Self-acceptance is your enriched fuel for launch!

DAY 1—BECOMING AN OVERCOMER

Becoming an overcomer is not an action, but an identity.

Becoming an overcomer is about *being* rather than *doing*. Living an overcoming life is not about fabricating a new persona or wearing a brave mask. Instead, becoming an overcomer means *being the authentic you*.

Tenacity, proactivity, and other traits shared by overcomers are part of your identity as a human being. It is no accident that you have made it this far; you are still standing because you were built to last. You were designed to overcome the obstacles in your path by using your human qualities to develop solutions and press toward your goals.

Your native strengths were evident at the moment of your birth. You were thrust from the comforts of the womb into an unfamiliar new world. Yet, as tiny and seemingly helpless as you were, you took your place on planet Earth and drew your first breath. When you were hungry, you advocated for yourself with the tools at your disposal; you cried, and loudly.

You were created, not to merely survive, but to thrive, and you knew it instinctively. You are a being built for freedom. You were factory-equipped with the power of your imagination and the emotional tuning necessary to surmount circumstances and perceived limitations with authority.

Even a lifelong history of hiding cannot lord it over you forever. Not only are you able to recover from that experience and move on, but you are also scheduled to launch from the edge and overcome it altogether. This is not about fishing around for improvised methods of behavior modification; it is a matter of unwrapping the totality of your authentic identity.

The real you has no desire to hide and every reason to stand tall—right out in the open.

CLASSIFIED ACTION—DAY 1

Ask yourself the following questions:

1. How do I see myself? (Consider the thoughts, words, and images that come to mind and write them down. Avoid self-editing, self-protecting, and creating new masks.)

2. Who am I? Who am I not? (This is not a test that you can fail. Relax and explore your identity with candor.)

3. What feelings arise as I ponder these questions? (Your feelings are valid and valuable; so don't become alarmed if they're not all pretty.)

DAY 2—KNOWING WHAT YOU WANT

Knowing what you want is not a head-trip; knowing what you want begins with recognizing the desires of your heart.

There is a biblical idea that addresses a universal experience: the all-too-common disparity between what we want and what we have. The Scriptures get straight to the point, saying, "...You do not have, because you do not ask."[1]

This stunning statement assumes that before you can pursue your desires in earnest, you have to know what they are. That may appear to be a statement of the obvious, but most of us have not developed or committed to a well-defined idea of what we want out of life.

We catch glimpses of our dreams on TV, in other people's lives, in books, and in our daydreams, but these are mostly vicarious ideas that pop in and out of our conscious thoughts without inspiring a course of action.

Building the life you want starts with the development of a clear picture. This image does not spring from a purely intellectual sense of what your life *should* be; the sense of what *should* be is often distorted by the presence of unmet needs. The picture of the life you desire originates in the core of your being and reveals your unadulterated desires.

In the case of the strong person hiding, these desires can be suppressed so effectively as to be completely forgotten. Is that your story? Has your childhood dream been banished to the recesses of the throw-away room and obscured from conscious memory?

Almost without exception, everyone has a dream that has been tossed aside. Yet, your dream can be unearthed by *allowing* the memory to resurface. You were created with the mental capacity to imagine your future and to describe how you would feel living it. In your mind's eye, you can see the details and mentally step into the picture to the point of being able to engage the sensations associated with it.

Envisioning your dreams will lead you to another important corridor of thought that begins with the following question: *Who will I need to become in order to be able to embrace my dream?* The process of becoming the star of your dream begins with your taking ownership of past choices and outcomes experienced so far.

Reconciling yourself with the past in this way releases you to enter the future while leaving old baggage behind. Then you can consider ways in which to prepare yourself to live in a new way. You will become aware of the character traits and mindsets needed to support your new life.

Knowing what you want is *powerful* and will lead you to what you need.

CLASSIFIED ACTION—DAY 2

The edge—where you are right now—does not have to be your endpoint. You are worthy of attaining your desires, and no one can pinpoint them better than you can.

1. Pause and quietly imagine what your ideal life would look like. Engage your senses so that the picture comes alive in your mind. Describe the images in writing, recording all of the details. Keep your description handy, and refer to it often.

2. Describe in detail where you are right now—how does your life look and feel? How do you see yourself in this life? What are you experiencing there?

3. Write a paragraph about who you would need to become in order to live the life you described in answer to question 1. What traits and mindsets will serve you well?

4. Focus on one area of life, such as health, finances, or career, and explore the following:

   a. Choices made and outcomes already experienced

   b. Choices yet to be made and the outcomes you desire

   c. Character traits and beliefs you believe will sustain your capacity to enjoy these results

---

DAY 3—EXPOSING ENERGY-ZAPPERS

Acknowledging and attending to life's low-level "pains" will free up your energy for more productive pursuits.

There are roses along the pathway to your dreams, but where there are roses, there are also thorns. One does not exist without the other. Likewise, every dream has a dream-blocker that comes with the territory. These "thorns" come in three main varieties: energy-zappers, unmet needs, and fears. Today we'll explore energy-zappers.

Not all energy-zappers come in large, conspicuous packages. We easily recognize the big ones, and because they are so obvious, we tend to deal with them promptly. Yet, we often tolerate or ignore altogether the subtle detractors that wear us down incrementally over time. These nuisances seem so inconsequential that we are blinded to their cumulative ability to distract us, muddy our vision, and drain our resources.

Energy-zappers come in many forms:

- Household clutter

- Squeaky doors

- Unfinished projects

- Broken promises

- Malfunctioning cars, electronics, or appliances

These pests grate on us day in and day out, much like the achy tooth you tolerate until the pain becomes so excruciating that an emergency dental appointment must be made.

This tendency to absorb chronic pain and inconvenience is costly. Energy-zappers slowly pile up and methodically wear you down. Dealing with them is a whole lot easier than tolerating them. Most energy-zappers don't require much attention to begin with and oftentimes, taking care of one pest helps to eliminate two or three others. Whether you choose to delegate or tackle the offender yourself, dealing with it will quickly defuse the emotional charge every energy-zapper carries—and the sooner you defuse it, the better!

Look around the room in which you are sitting right now. Are there two or three energy-zappers staring you in the face? Maybe it's the remote control with the volume button that always sticks, the reading lamp that doesn't throw enough light, or the patio screen that doesn't close properly. Stop and think about how many times these pests have drawn your attention or your ire.

Is tolerating them giving you anything worth having—and what are they costing you?

CLASSIFIED ACTION—DAY 3

Today is the day to expose the energy-zappers in your life and put them on notice that you won't be tolerating them anymore!

1. With pen and notebook in hand, do a walk-through in your home and in your workplace. Examine your car, too. List every energy-zapper you see.

2. Every one of these items that continues to hang over you has a cost. Determine what it is costing you to leave this item unaddressed. Include in your calculation any losses in terms of frustration, safety, worry, disappointment to others, collateral damage, and financial cost.

3. What does your inattention to the energy-zappers communicate about your sense of self-worth?

4. What is one action step you can take in each of these cases, and how will taking that step make you feel?

DAY 4—MEETING UNMET NEEDS

Having needs is an essential human trait; acknowledging and addressing them fosters humility and emotional health.

Imagine a sturdy bucket with a hole in it. Now picture what happens when you try to fill it with enough water to perform gardening or cleaning tasks fifty feet away from the water source. No matter how high you fill the bucket, how fast you run, or what makeshift remedies you apply, the water you need to accomplish your goal will find its way out, and the bucket will be soon be empty again.

Emotionally speaking, unmet needs work in much the same way. We feel empty when our basic human needs go unaddressed. Until we are willing to acknowledge these dream-blocking needs and find healthy ways in which to meet them, we will try plugging up the hole and filling the bucket with counterfeit forms of the approval, safety, esteem, and fulfillment of potential we rightfully crave.

Most of this activity occurs on an unconscious level. That is where our unmet needs drive our behavior along the unhealthy avenues we hope will provide at least temporary fulfillment. These unmet needs often masquerade as healthy, legitimate requirements. These legitimate human needs fall under four basic categories:

- The need for security
- The need for power and influence
- The need for achievement
- The need for relationship.

When subjected to closer examination, unhealthy needs reveal a distortion that warrants suspicion. These distortions are not so difficult to spot; they include obsessive and compulsive desires, excessive neediness, co-dependency, and other damaging behaviors. Unmet needs are also revealed in a variety of emotions, such as frustration, fearfulness, disappointment, hurt, anger, or the sense that we are in some way incomplete.

Unmet needs can be distinguished from healthy ones by the pressing demands they place upon us: when we are being played by our unmet needs, we believe that we cannot live them. Therefore, we seek frequent "refills," and we seek them incessantly.

Grant yourself the freedom to have your legitimate needs met and your unmet needs resolved—and enjoy the fulfillment that is yours for the asking.

CLASSIFIED ACTION—DAY 4

Your needs and the meeting of your needs are essential in becoming your biggest self and living your biggest life. So, pick up your pen and notebook and say goodbye to that empty feeling!

1. Get flat-out honest with yourself and make a list of your top ten needs, then decide whether you prefer to list them in any particular order of importance.

2. Use an asterisk to mark the needs that you believe have gone unmet. List some healthy ways in which you can meet those needs. (Example: If you feel isolated due to unmet relational needs, you might consider becoming involved in a cooking club or church group.)

3. Identify, in writing, the signs you feel are pointing to these as unmet needs. How have those identifying features played out in your life outcomes so far?

4. How will meeting these needs in healthier ways promote more desirable outcomes? Be specific.

DAY 5— FINDING THE HANDLE ON YOUR FEAR

Already resident within is the courage to turn fear to your advantage. Fear is the opportunity your courage has been waiting for.

Fear is the third dream-blocker. An anonymous legend demonstrates powerfully the fact that it is not fear itself but our interpretation of fear that produces adverse results.

"One day a man was wandering in the desert when he met Fear and Plague. They said they were on their way to a large city where they were going to kill 10,000 people. The man asked Plague if he was going to do all the work. Plague smiled and said, 'No, I'll only take care of a few hundred. I'll let my friend Fear do the rest.'"[2]

In Chapter 7, we discovered that courage is not the absence of fear, but the decision to act in spite of, and in the presence of, fear. Without fear, courage cannot exist, and the only power fear holds over us is the power to deceive us into expecting the worst. When we are tricked into perceiving fear-based images as equivalent to reality, we can undo ourselves without any outside help.

You needn't buy in to fear's beckoning. You were born to be a champion over fear. Champions don't wait for fear to determine their outcomes; champions *decide* what their outcomes will be. These life-defining decisions are made in the face of fear; they are made by going eyeball to eyeball with fear and turning it to your advantage.

Imagine that you are an astronaut strapped in for launch. You have butterflies in your stomach. You are turbo-charged with excitement; the energy is racing through your body and facilitating alert responses to the rush of signals and commands that accompany every launch.

As the nation watches the countdown on television, untold thousands are thinking about how frightening it would be to sit in your chair. Meanwhile, you are imagining how awesome it will be to feel those rockets fire beneath you as you leave Earth's atmosphere to see the wonders of space right outside your window.

Fear produces the same energy that excitement does. It is energy you can use to serve your purpose. First you must decide whether you will be the astronaut or the fearful spectator. The story you tell yourself will determine how high you will fly.

CLASSIFIED ACTION—DAY 5

There is no better time than now to turn the tables on fear and make it your servant. Be determined to reclaim lost turf and never again yield back so much as one inch of it to fear.

1. Focus on a particular situation or opportunity about which you have some trepidation and ask yourself the following questions:

   a. Exactly what am I afraid of? Is it something I fear will happen? Am I worried about what someone will think or say about me? Is there something I fear losing forever?

   b. What is the worst possible outcome, and what will that outcome mean to me?

   c. Is this fear rooted in an old story I am accustomed to telling myself? Is the story based in truth?

2. Consider a pattern of fear that you have experienced over time (For instance: Perhaps you regularly avoid group settings because you feel insecure in that kind of interaction.) How can you reframe your thoughts and beliefs to break this pattern of fear? What will you gain by doing so?

3. What new stories can you tell yourself about your posture in relation to fear-producing situations or events? How can your new stories create the emotional environment that will reveal the champion within?

_____

CHAM·PI·ON

- One that wins first place or first prize in a competition.

- One that is clearly superior or has the attributes of a winner: *a champion at teaching.*

- An ardent defender or supporter of a cause or another person: *a champion of the homeless.*

- One who fights; a warrior.[3]

CALLING ALL CHAMPIONS!

These five days have been your opportunity to enter into the kind of growth spurt that can change the very atmosphere of your life. My hope and my prayer are for you to have drained every last drop of potential these days have offered you. If you have, you are ready to drink in the next five days' worth!

Before you move on, let's take a quick look at the qualities of a champion— the champion within who is in the process of being unleashed.

Champions determine outcomes. Champions are can-do people. They don't play "wait and see" with their results in life. Instead, they play a formative role in the achievement of their outcomes. They do this by determining within themselves what their outcomes will be. They follow through by making the choices and taking the actions that will support the outcomes they have already envisioned. Champions approach outcomes this way in part because they have discovered the courage that is resident within them. When fear speaks, champions choose to consider fear within the context of their available courage.

Champions value the edge and see its potential as a launch pad. The champion transforms fear into excitement and then draws upon the energy the excitement yields. Champions realize that every life is marked by "edge" experiences. They understand that those experiences are valuable opportunities to launch into a bigger life; they are also aware that to waste an opportunity is to ensure loss.

Champions accept responsibility and hold themselves accountable. Champions do not fear taking responsibility because they believe in their ability and worthiness to live a big life. For them, responsibility is a portion of the fair price of success; they would rather pay up front than suffer disappointing outcomes later. They know that holding themselves accountable for their choices, actions, and results is the only way to be sure that they are meeting their responsibilities.

Champions are internally driven. Champions don't expect other people or outside stimuli to motivate them. They listen to and are driven by the causes, desires, and passions of their own hearts. They are goal-oriented people of vision who are decisive in part because they know what they want. They do not yield to every passing fad or bow their knees to externally imposed pressures to perform, think, or act in popular ways. They are centered on truth, and they allow truth to guide them.

You are a champion, and you've been called to greatness. Now it's time to turn the page; you've got five big days ahead!

Chapter 12

REFRAME YOUR FOUNDATION IN 10 DYNAMIC DAYS
DAYS 6–10

"Live out of your imagination, not your history."
—Stephen Covey

ONCE you are settled into the assurance that, regardless of your age or history, you can choose a more promising future, your sense of the past changes—radically. Instead of being burdened by remorse or deceived by denial, you are free to remember the past without being controlled by it.

Kept in perspective, your past experiences have continuing value. However their merit is not in their ability to predict what's next; they are significant because they help propel you to the edge—your launch pad—the place where you can look forward with greater wisdom, hope, and determination.

With five dynamic days of your foundation reframe still fresh in your mind, you have five terrific days yet ahead! Make the most of them. Glean all you can from your past experiences so that you can create a fabulous future. Own what you have learned, and own what you can do with the knowledge and insight you have gained. When you do, your personal foundation will provide the hope, grace, and resiliency you once believed were out of your reach.

Step right up to a bigger life; it is entirely within your grasp. The strides you have already taken prove it. For one, you have poked holes through the bubble of fear and misbelief that once enveloped you as a strong person hiding. At the same time, you have begun the process of replacing the weak links in your framework so that you can build upon your foundation with confidence...and build *any* life you have the imagination to design.

Don't stop now—keep pressing in. There's more freedom yet ahead!

Day 6—Making Room for the Real You

Creating the life you want means making room for the emotional inventory your new life requires.

By now you have developed some distinct ideas about what you want from life and what you don't. This is monumental, because the instant you become consciously aware of your preferences (even before the picture is rendered completely clear), your internal momentum shifts. Instead of heartfelt, purpose-driven desires yielding to the seemingly uncontrolled circumstances of your life, you and your desires have climbed into the driver's seat, and *you have taken the wheel.*

Having regained command of your life, this fact remains: Life is about choices, and there are more decisions yet to be made. Some of the old infrastructure that supported the hiding lifestyle is probably still in place, although just barely. It is time for a clean sweep; old paradigms take up valuable space, and you need that space to complete your reframe.

To clear the space you need, become an astute observer of yourself. Carefully survey your internal landscape and search out any straggling dream-blockers. Don't tiptoe around them; evict them! This will prevent them from undermining the momentum shift that is already in progress.

A key part of your internal structure is your self-talk. Re-scan your internal monologue for any signs of the words, images, memories, and thoughts that once supported shame—low self-worth, self-sabotage, mistaken identities, and any other hiding mechanisms. When you detect an offender, deal with it. Don't entertain emotional clutter; be finished with it once and for all.

If old thoughts beg for a stay of execution—and especially if you are tempted to tolerate them—take a measurement. Stand them up against the outcomes you desire and ask yourself this question: *Will this element of my self-talk help me to achieve my desired outcomes, or will it compromise or even cost me my dreams?*

The question will practically answer itself.

Ar·bi·ter

- A person empowered to decide matters at issue; judge; umpire.

- A person who has the sole or absolute power of judging or determining.[2]

CLASSIFIED ACTION—DAY 6

Become the willful arbiter of your self-talk—and take no prisoners! Hold court over every word and image that plays out in your mind. You have control over the tape that plays there: arrest, erase, and re-record any content that stands in defiance of your dreams.

1. Take five minutes each day to stop and listen to your self-talk. Or double the time to ten minutes if you'd like to experience an even more noticeable momentum shift.

2. Write down what you are hearing and seeing in your self-talk. Don't be intimidated by content you find unsettling. You have to acknowledge its existence in order to effect its eviction!

3. As you record your self-talk in writing, decide which words, phrases, and images properly define the real you and which ones need to be re-recorded (reframed).

4. Follow-through on the reframe by writing down and/or describing the words, phrases, and images that you will choose to replace the old self-talk. (Each time the old thoughts pop up, you'll need to consciously replace them with the new ones.)

5. How do these adjustments help to redefine you?

6. What other choices can you make in support of these changes?

Day 7—Changing Your Perspective

Your vantage point is always subject to change and can impact your outlook in surprising ways.

Have you ever taken an online tour of a home layout? You can usually select from a series of still shots in which individual rooms are seen from a particular vantage point in the home. These stills provide a limited view of each room, but what they cannot provide is a realistic sense of how the rooms flow into one another and how it feels to walk through the home.

Sometimes, you can take a 360-degree virtual tour. By clicking and dragging the cursor, you can select views from every conceivable angle. As you move from left to right and from bottom to top, the room glides around you. As it does, you see things that were not visible in the stills and you get a more complete understanding of the layout of the home.

Life is not static; it is fluid. The situations in our lives are changeable. Just as you can't get the feel of a house from a still shot, you can't develop a comprehensive perspective of your life from a single viewpoint. When contrary circumstances seem immoveable, you can choose to see them differently, simply by changing your vantage point.

Consider an example common to student life: An instructor assigns a term paper of significant length on what seems to be a challenging topic. Students have four weeks to complete the project; their results will significantly impact their final grades.

If you're not currently in the midst of such an experience, imagine that you are. Now picture the term paper in the way that students often do—as a steep, craggy mountain that has just been dropped onto your path. When you stand at the base of the mountain and look up, the size of the mountain can overwhelm you. The peak seems out of reach, and the terrain looks threatening.

Getting started is difficult because your perspective has blown the size of the project out of all proportion.

Yet, once you get started, you begin to gain momentum and confidence. Suddenly, part of the mountain is below you, and the distance to the top seems manageable. The mountain doesn't seem nearly as massive as it did before. As you gather your research and begin to draft parts of your paper, you see it coming together. You might even find yourself becoming interested in the subject. Before you know it, you're looking forward to your turn-in date because you are anticipating a good grade.

What changed? Only your perspective! When it comes to a point of view, or even your worldview, the most subtle shift in your position can bring a profound change in your attitude and approach—to life, relationships, contrary circumstances, and even your expectations.

If you have ever talked to people who got a second chance at life following a catastrophic illness, near-fatal accident, or even a period of imprisonment, you have probably noticed a change in their approach to life. They don't sweat the small stuff as much as they used to; they may even be more forgiving and merciful than they were in the past.

That someone may be you or someone you care about. Whatever the case may be, you can see how powerful a change in perspective can be. The good news is that you don't have to wait for a traumatic event to thrust a new perspective upon you; you can change your vantage point anytime you choose to do so.

Today is as good a day as any.

CLASSIFIED ACTION—DAY 7

Changing your point of view can transform a situation or relationship; ultimately, it can transform your life. Become aware of your current perspective(s), and be open to some new ones. You may be surprised by the result!

1. Consider two situations or circumstances you assess as being adverse. Briefly describe these examples in writing. Frame your descriptions as a reporter would; include the important facts pertaining to who, what, when, where, why, and how.

2. For each example, describe your vantage point—the position from which you perceive and the way in which you perceive—the situation or circumstance. Where helpful, use prepositions (such as above, beneath, in, under, over) and adjectives (such as daunting, damaging, huge, devastating, perplexing) to aid your description.

3. Add to each answer from question 2 an explanation of what emotions you experience from the described vantage point.

4. For each situation or circumstance, list at least one alternate vantage point you might choose. How would seeing the situation differently affect your feelings about the issue? How might your changed feelings affect actual outcomes?

5. If you still feel stuck in your perspective, explain the ways in which you feel locked in. Is your "stuckness" externally or internally imposed? Can you identify any misbeliefs that might be operating? How can reframing these misbeliefs help to un-jam you?

DAY 8—BEING EMPOWERED BY PURPOSE

When you pinpoint your purpose, you are empowered to live from your being, and you are freed from the tyranny of doing for the wrong reasons.

The idea of purpose is a popular one in contemporary culture—and with good reason. Your purpose is an integral element of your authentic identity, and when it is integrated into the conduct of your life, it is empowering in extreme ways.

Purpose is a cornerstone of your foundation; it gives your life meaning, structure, and context. When your purpose is known, your desires become self-evident. You know what you want, and you know why you want it. Because your wants are based on your purpose, there is no question of impure motives, and there is no guilt in prosperity. Your *having* springs not from unmet needs but from your *being*.

As a person grounded in purpose, you will not spend precious days wondering where you're headed. You'll be spared of fishing around for a direction because your path will be clear. The clarity that is spawned by a sense of purpose is a self-perpetuating benefit: the more engaged you are with your purpose, the clearer your direction becomes.

Rabbit trails rarely distract purpose-driven people. When purpose is your motivator, choices become distinct; confidence and decisiveness flourish; and time-wasters are more easily avoided. Questions that once perplexed now resolve themselves. People who once perplexed no longer have the power to derail you.

When your life is guided by purpose, you will not suffer the emptiness that asks, "Is that all there is?" You will realize that transparency is not to be feared, but embraced. Being known by others won't seem threatening, but rewarding. Mistaken identities will become unappealing. Happiness and joy won't be exclusively attached to a desired destination, but will be experienced in the journey, too. Life's milestones will take on added meaning.

With your purpose lodged in your heart, you will find yourself being the person you were created to be, doing what you love to do, and having what you want to have...for all the right reasons.

CLASSIFIED ACTION—DAY 8

Although life's difficulties can serve to obscure your purpose for a time, you are, in actuality, inseparable from your purpose. Unveiling it anew or more fully can introduce a fresh vitality to your life.

1. If you have found it difficult to articulate your life's purpose, take several minutes to access your ideas. Allow yourself to free associate; rather than trying to direct your thoughts, allow them to spring to mind. Be ready to jot down, without self-editing, whatever words or phrases come to mind. What do your notes reveal?

2. Make a simple list of the ten things you most love to do. Don't worry about arranging them in any particular order; focus on the ten activities and pursuits that bring you the most joy and satisfaction.

3. When your answer to question 2 is complete, consider the ten items on your list. What do you think makes these pursuits so fulfilling? Write down your thoughts. Also write down any ideas as to how your answers may be pointing to your life's purpose.

4. Imagine your life's final outcomes; write your own eulogy and then read it.

5. How does your eulogy affect and/or motivate you?

DAY 9—CELEBRATING YOUR VALUES

Values are the habits of your heart, the silent sentinels guarding your choices and actions.

What you value reflects a belief that runs to the core of your being; it is part of what makes you a completely unique creation. Assuming that your unmet needs have been resolved, your core values will prove to be the primary drivers of your life. Knowing what is important to you—what your values are—is a critical aspect of knowing and being yourself.

Especially in light of today's climate of relativism and shifting mores, the act of living a value-centered life is a radical one. More and more, Western culture seems to be based in the self-centeredness that fosters the following beliefs:

- Whatever I believe—or want to believe—is truth.

- Whatever brings me pleasure is good.

- Whatever works in my situation is right.

- Whatever it takes to get what I want is acceptable.

Living a value-centered life lifts one's perspective to a higher plane where truth underlies moral choices and concern for the well-being of others is always a pressing factor. Value-centeredness speaks this way:

- Truth determines my beliefs.

- I will find the greatest satisfaction in doing the right things for the right reasons.

- Doing what is right will improve my situation in the long run.

- If my desires push me to do what I know in my heart is wrong, then my desires are suspect.

When I can articulate my values and am committed to being true to them, I am living in support of my authentic identity. When I set my values aside for the sake of expediency, I disconnect what I do from who I am. In order to enable my identity disconnect, I must necessarily become invisible. This invisibility will force me to assume future mistaken identities.

When I fail to honor my values, the resulting disconnect from self is not limited to spiritual and emotional levels. It can manifest in my physical life as well. For example, if I value good health but I am careless about nutritional choices and inattentive to fitness, I am living in conflict with my values. My overall health will eventually reflect the contradiction: my vitality will be diminished, my weight will become an issue, and my health will be compromised.

Living in conflict with your core values fosters a pervasive sense of confusion and therefore, frustration. Because the conflict requires us to become opaque and deny our true selves, we become unable to identify the source of our confusion. Instead of having our efforts rewarded with satisfaction, we become increasingly discontented with life and more susceptible to a shame-based identity.

To celebrate your values is to honor and validate your authentic identity.

CLASSIFIED ACTION—DAY 9

We demonstrate our values through our attitudes and behaviors. Often, others see our values in action more clearly than we do. Recognizing on a conscious level the values we hold dear is an important step in achieving wholeness.

1. Reflect on the qualities that were seen in you during your childhood years (ages six through twelve). List them. Which of those qualities represent your core values? How so?

2. What would your life look like if your work, time expenditures, and other involvements were more consistently aligned with the qualities listed in answer to question 1?

3. Describe five specific instances in the past two to five years when you felt you were at your best; that is, your being and doing were in synch with your values. How did you feel at those times? How did those experiences differ from others?

4. Name two activities or pursuits no one would be able to stop you from doing. Explain how these activities or pursuits are aligned with your core values.

5. Examine your current workweek. Explain how your core values are expressed through your work and schedule. Describe any values that are as yet unexpressed in your work.

DAY 10—MAKING AND LIVING YOUR RULES

Empowerment is not about power at all; it is about ownership—owning, releasing, and focusing one's energy toward a desired outcome.

We are works in progress. With every breath, we involuntarily advance toward life's chronological finish line—the day when, whether we have lived our dreams or not, the physical clock will stop ticking.

Until then, we have 86,400 seconds each day in which we can choose to move toward the destiny finish line. This is not a physical endpoint; it is the outcome in which the fulfillment of our lives has been experienced. It is the place where chronological measurements are inconsequential; the moments that bring us here are the taking of ownership, the submission to accountability, the development of persistence and focus, and the working of grace.

Life never occurs in a vacuum. Instead, whether it is convenient or not, life occurs on multiple tracks that run concurrently. So often, in our frantic efforts to keep up, we take from Peter and give to Paul to the extent that we lose sight of our focal points. We wind up improvising our way through each day, and if we're not careful, we construct new hiding places to help us deal with the pressure. This is the nature of survival-mode living.

Here's a news flash—your days of survival mode are in the past, and so are mine! Although it is easy to slip back into old patterns, it isn't all that hard to prevent a costly relapse. It is a matter of being consistent by keeping your desired outcomes in sight and conducting your life in ways that are compatible with those outcomes.

Day 10 is a milestone; it is your day to distill what you know, what you want, and what you can do to five simple rules. These rules should be tailored to your situation and designed to create accountability for the life you choose to live.

As you develop these five rules, use the resources already at your disposal. You have lots of information and personal development from which you can draw:

1. *The "top ten" lists from Chapter 10, including the hallmarks of your biggest self, and the keys to your biggest life.* The hallmarks are foundational qualities to develop and strengthen. The keys are a set of guidelines that promote transparency, a posture of power, and the transformation of life's "edges" into launch pads.

2. *The growth steps you have taken over the past nine days and the journaling you have done.* These are terrific reference points; they

highlight key areas of your life and contribute to the development of your big picture.

3.   *Your purpose and the clarification it provides about your place in the world.* Knowing why you're here helps you to prioritize and shape your choices and actions so they are productive and aligned with your purpose.

4.   *Your goals, dreams, and desires, especially within the context of your life's purpose.* Knowing what you want to achieve and have (and why you want to achieve/have it) helps you to avoid wasting time and energy on activities that cannot produce what you want.

5.   *Your values and vision.* These provide guidance and structure, respectively, so that you not only achieve your desired outcomes, but you do so in ways that are honoring to you, to others, and to your life's purpose.

6.   Your understanding of the specific issues and attitudes that drove you into hiding (especially within the context of new attitudes that support your desired outcomes). Having a clear sense of the difference between self-sabotaging patterns and self-honoring ones will prevent backsliding into comfort zones that serve only to undermine you.

7.   *The establishment and recognition of healthy boundaries.* Forming and observing healthy boundaries will help you to develop relationships that support, rather than oppose, your desired outcomes.

8.   *Your intellectual acuity, spiritual beliefs, creative abilities, and other strengths.* There is a wealth of understanding, wisdom, and talent resident within you!

CLASSIFIED ACTION—DAY 10

You have the background you need to establish five simple, personal rules. These will serve as a strategic guidance system upon which you can rely even as circumstances and situations change in the years to come.

Following are five tips to help you in composing your five rules.

1. Base these rules upon your internal motivations of what you want to do rather than what feel you should do.

2. Make these rules your own; they should be more specific to your life than to anyone else's.

3. Think big picture and long term. At the same time, realize that your needs may change over time. Updating your rules later is perfectly acceptable.

4. Consider inviting a trusted friend or other significant person to offer feedback and hold you accountable to your rules. Offer to do the same for them. Interaction should be nonjudgmental and objective. Finger pointing, nagging, and defensiveness are out of line and counterproductive.

5. Keep your rules on an index card for handy reference. You'll be amazed at how often they will provide the answers you need in future situations.

10 DAYS STRONGER

You did it! You took ten days—ten giant steps—toward a better, stronger, more functional personal foundation. From where you sit right now, you can't see the full impact of your efforts, but I can assure you that the residual effects of these ten days will prove significant over the months and years to come.

Your reframe has created the sturdy infrastructure you need to accommodate the big life that is ahead of you. No—the work is not yet complete; your biggest life can still only be lived one day at a time. It will require your ongoing commitment to freedom and your faithful diligence in sticking with it—in refusing to slip back into a fearful and shame-based life. That's what your five rules are for: they are reminders of where you are going and of the road that will take you there.

So, stand tall in your God-given strength and in your persistence to become *every bit* the woman or man you were created to be. Love the edge you're standing on, and take it boldly. Look in the mirror and turn the page.

The authentic you is about to make his or her mark on the world!

Conclusion

YOU ARE AN ABSOLUTE WONDER!

"The purpose of life is to live it, to taste experience to the utmost, to reach out eagerly and without fear for newer and richer experience."
—Eleanor Roosevelt

YOU'RE not Wonder Woman or Superman—you are more amazing than that. You are the real thing, a living, breathing person of stunning strengths and outstanding ability. You are truly a marvel.

If a question is rising to your lips at this moment, it's probably this: *But, Terri, how can you say that if we've never even met?* It's a great question, one that has arisen before in one form or another as you have read the pages of this book.

That is why I am so eager to answer it one more time. My response could not be more personal if you and I were talking over lunch or enjoying a day together. I could not believe it more or state it more sincerely, because the truth is the truth any way you slice it.

So here's what I want to say to you right now, and through the power of print, as many times as you need to hear it in the days to come:

You are one wonder of a person! From the inside out, you are divinely created—an unequaled masterpiece, a multi-faceted gem so unique as to be beyond priceless, a powerhouse of potential ready to explode on the scene with a combination of abilities and qualities no one can duplicate. You have made it this far, you have come through so much, and you have so much life and joy ahead. Thinking of it gives me chills, because I know that...

Your potential is more expansive than the boundless sky.

Nothing can stop you (except you) and you've come too far to stop yourself now.

Everything you have been, done, and experienced has led you here, and from here you can go anyplace in life that you choose!

I could go on and on about you, but this is your time to do the talking. You have a lot to say with the rest of your life.

Your Toolbox Is Ready

Anyone who has ever married or become pregnant with a first child has experienced cold feet. You can be dating for years, longing for the day when Mr. Right will pop the question. When he does, you wear the ring proudly, and you look forward to the day the two of you will wed.

Yet, invariably there comes a moment of fear. You wonder whether you're ready for marriage or whether you're marrying the right guy. The same is true as you face parenthood. You wonder how in the world you will measure up to the responsibility of caring for your new baby and raising your child to become a loving, responsible adult.

If you can relate to doubts like these, you're in the company of several billion people who have entertained similar concerns throughout centuries of human existence. Yet, in spite of their butterflies, couples marry every day, and babies continue to be born all over the world.

Doubt and trepidation are part of the human experience. You will probably encounter some form of the jitters each time you approach life's latest edge. That's just the way it goes.

The difference is that you're no longer stuck there, shivering as you stand frozen on the edge. You have got all kinds of assets, and these assets are your tools. You were born with these tools in your toolbox, and you've been polishing them up. You know how to remodel the edge and transform it into your launch pad, and you *know* that you can fly as high as you want to!

Let's check out five key assets, or tools, that are always at your disposal:

You are a strong person who values the integrity of your internal structure. Your internal structure includes your beliefs, attitudes, thoughts, habits, intellect, feelings, and identity. It is the framework of your life; it upholds you and guides your choices and actions.

Your diligence to reframe your internal structure is affecting the whole of your life. Instead of allowing your thought life to fly under the radar undetected, unsupervised, and unquestioned, you have retaken command by exercising your power to choose.

You have discovered the scripts and postures that are affecting your life and you are challenging them. You have become aware of your self-talk, and you are equipped to revise it as needed. You have assessed your gait, and you understand its importance. You know the difference between a victim mindset and the posture of power, and you recognize the implications of both.

You have discovered the value of knowing who you are and what you want. You're not suspicious or ashamed of your desires because you know how to evaluate your motives. You can tell the difference between the patterns driven by unmet needs and the desires that are aligned with your purpose. You know that, to live fully, your purpose will be at the center of all you do.

You are a strong person who embraces transparency and your authentic identity. You are no longer under the wrap of fear. Neither are you caught in the tension of opposing tendencies—wanting others to pass by without noticing you, but suffering the pain of your invisibility.

You have confronted fear and laid bare the root of shame. Any layers of mistaken identity that have been developed as coping mechanisms—the very cover-ups that contributed to your painful invisibility—have been exposed and peeled away. You are no longer hiding; you are willing to be known, and you are comfortable with being knowable.

You have discovered the value of authenticity and are better able to accept yourself, imperfections and all. No longer are you pressed into a performance mentality designed to garner the approval and affirmation of others. You have come to grips with the idea that you are not a human *doing*, but a human *being*, an individual whose value is inherent rather than earned.

Because you recognize your inestimable worth, you are becoming increasingly comfortable with your needs as a human being. You realize that your needs are as valid as anyone else's, and you are transparent enough to have your needs met. You are able to identify any remaining unmet needs, and you are choosing *not* to be driven by them.

Transparency and authenticity have made room for your strengths to flourish and for your authentic, fulfilling life to unfold.

You are a strong person who demonstrates an ownership mentality. The fact that you are empowered is evident, not in displays of might, but in the taking of responsibility for your choices and in your willingness to be held accountable for them.

You have exited the throwaway room on your own power; you are not waiting for someone to rescue you. Nor do you seek safety in being controlled. You see yourself as the one who is best suited and most fully equipped to chart your own course in life.

Because your choices are your own, you have the freedom to match your choices with compatible actions. You are less afraid of making a mistake than you are of doing nothing at all. Your freedom to act creates an environment in which you can choose your outcomes and take the steps needed to achieve them.

With each success (and even when you experience a setback), you own your role and your outcomes. Through each experience, you are growing stronger and more confident of who you are and what you can do.

You have discovered that you are not called to condemn yourself for your mistakes or missteps. Instead, you are willing to forgive yourself so that you can make better choices in the future. By responding in this way, you correctly honor your being and the person you are becoming.

Because you have an ownership mentality, your happiness does not rest in the hands of others, and your failures cannot promote shame. Instead, you recognize that every circumstance is a growth opportunity and a testimony of continued progress.

In the long run, we shape our lives, and we shape ourselves. The process never ends until we die. And the choices we make are ultimately our own responsibility.[2]

—Eleanor Roosevelt

You are a strong person who establishes healthy boundaries and supports their observance. You know where you begin and end. You are a person with a purpose, able to command your space in the world. Your identity is becoming more clearly defined, and you appreciate the importance of honoring and respecting yourself first in order to be honored and respected by others.

Your regard for healthy boundaries stems from your understanding of their purpose in clarifying personal identity and responsibility. You willingly accept your responsibilities; at the same time, you are unwilling to accept or impose misplaced guilt or blame in order to gain approval or remain invisible.

You are better able to distinguish between appropriate and inappropriate forms of interaction; therefore, you are positioned to assess the content of your interaction with others. You are proactive in training others to treat you appropriately. They respect your intolerance of detrimental behaviors. More and more, they value and respect your authentic identity because they can see that you do.

You avail yourself of the freedom to redefine at any time as a means of shedding mistaken and self-sabotaging identities. This redefinition engages your power to choose, act, and achieve results. It also enables you to restore boundaries that may have been eroded by passivity or the inappropriate intrusions of others.

The identification of your core values has made you better able to define beneficial boundaries. Because your established boundaries are congruent with your core values, you are neither confused nor tentative in enforcing them.

Due to the increased clarity your values provide, you can no longer be deceived by the subtleties of the slow boil. You are quick to recognize a breach in your boundaries and quick to call yourself and others to account in a gracious, loving, and assertive way.

You are a strong person who recognizes and seizes opportunity. Because you recognize your power to choose in every circumstance and situation, you have become more aware of the abundance of opportunity that is present in your life. You are not only aware of opportunity, but you also feel empowered to seize the opportunities that are aligned with your values, vision, and purpose.

As the four assets already mentioned continue to develop, you become increasingly aware of certain ongoing opportunities that are available to you as a matter of course. These include:

- *The opportunity to establish a life environment conducive to the support of your dreams.* When you reframe your internal structure, you seize the opportunity to strengthen your personal foundation and eliminate even subtle dream-blockers. Your seizure of this fundamental opportunity creates a climate of opportunity in every area of life.

- *The opportunity to become the person you were created to be.* When you embrace your authentic identity and seek to shed cover-ups, you seize the opportunity to become your biggest self and therefore, to enjoy your biggest life.

- *The opportunity to become an agent of change in your life and world.* When the taking of ownership becomes your lifestyle, your choices and actions yield further opportunities for favorable results. As an expression of your life's purpose, these results can have far-reaching effects.

- *The opportunity to engage in productive, life-giving relationships.* When you establish and observe healthy boundaries, you are seizing the opportunity to engage in mutually beneficial relationships with others. These relationships have the power to enhance your life and your outcomes.

The strong person takes a proactive approach to every opportunity, knowing that an opportunity exploited is a potential launch pad for his or her dreams.

Now that you have explored your toolbox, bear in mind that each of us is developing in different areas at varying rates of speed. My growth areas may not be identical to yours, yet we both have areas in our lives where we have room for improvement. Be patient with yourself, knowing that the journey is as important as the destination. In fact, you could say that the journey *is* the destination.

Become What You Believe

When I was hiding, I seemed to be standing still while the world moved past me. Practically speaking, it was true; I *was* parked on the sidelines in the race of life.

I had gradually become a spectator and had learned how *not* to be in the game. To stay on the sidelines, I had to suppress my desire to participate. My strengths as a person and even my physical abilities were cast aside; this was the price I paid to remain safely hidden from rejection and abandonment. I successfully smothered my identity to such a degree that I neutralized the very tools that qualified me to compete in the race of life.

It took every bit of my strength to subdue my natural proclivities and stay under cover. But the day came when the kettle of my suppressed emotions boiled over and the lid blew off. It was the day when I saw my first jet-ski race. As the machines flew by, carving the water and sending up swirls of spray, my arm shot straight up in an expression of glee from deep within me.

The deep waters of my heart had been stirred and were overflowing the banks of fear and shame. I heard my voice cry out: "I can do that! I identify with that!" I realized I was no longer willing to stand safely on the edge wearing the uniform of a bystander. I was supposed to be in the race. *I was born to be in the race!*

In that moment, I decided to do whatever it would take to learn the sport of jet-ski racing and to become a champion. You know the story—I had no clue how to handle the machine; I just kept trying. I would ride until my hands were raw. It was terrifying at times, but I found a way to turn the fear into excitement. I learned how to ride into the zone where the sport expressed my purpose and the machine and I became one.

I fully expected to hear the old, mocking voices saying:

"You're too big for your britches."

"Who said you could come out of nowhere and compete with the rest of us?"

"Who do you think you are, and what could you possibly accomplish?"

I had heard those voices all my life. But I had known since the night of my gutter experience that something was going to have to change. Now I'd found my opportunity to make it real, and before long, I had become the fastest female jet-ski racer on record.

I discovered a way to become what I believed I could be. It wasn't just about racing; it was about life. Somehow, by seizing the opportunity to get in the game, I began to discover my purpose. It was to inspire others to get in the game, to connect with their own hearts, to identify their unique contribution, and to make a difference in their lives and in their world.

My greatest desire is for you to become what *you* believe. Nothing would thrill me more than to hear people like you step up and say, "I can do that!" and then go ahead and *do it*.

In case you're still skeptical, let me tell one thing I know for sure: getting in the game is well within the realm of possibility. You will get there—one step at a time. And even if you pick up a bruise or two along the way, it will serve your purpose in the end.

A woman who is convinced that she deserves to accept only the best challenges herself to give the best. Then she is living phenomenally.[3]

—Maya Angelou

Brilliant by Birth

There is something else I want to leave with you; it is the longing for a depth of authenticity that releases an understanding of your native brilliance. This is a powerful realization that will outlast the moments of doubt and insecurity that inevitably come to every life.

When you begin to fathom the brilliance inherent within you, you begin to enjoy a level of freedom like none you've ever known. This knowledge breeds a level of self-confidence that can come only from the realization that even in your most insecure moments, the brilliance of others will not intimidate or detract from yours.

You will find yourself comfortably competing in the race of life and knowing that you occupy a unique place in the shared ground of human experience. Instead of fearing loss or seeing yourself from the "less than" perspective that once kept you hiding, you will become a conduit of impenetrable strength and emotional buoyancy that will elevate the prospects of others as it does your own.

As you become empowered day by day to live the life of your dreams, you will clearly see this truth: There is more than enough room on the planet for all of us to demonstrate the brilliance that radiates from within.

This knowledge has the power to release us from the need to jockey for advantage or position. Instead we are free to stand shoulder to shoulder with other people simultaneously honoring our shared humanity and unique identities.

This is the emotional place from which mutual trust develops and transparency thrives. It is where the need to undercut others or to place them on towering pedestals ends. It is where the need to self-protect by coming on strong or by wearing an insincere "nice" mask becomes unnecessary.

It is the emotional location from which you can place yourself in plain view of others and live as an overcomer. From this enviable position, you can reveal the fears that were once held secret, and you can share the knowledge you once felt compelled to keep for yourself. This is the land of liberation in which you are no longer invisible but completely transparent.

From this place of freedom, hiding becomes obsolete because we are no longer bound by classifications of *superior* or *subordinate*. In the absence of these distinctions, we freely give others and ourselves permission to make mistakes, take risks, and challenge the paradigms that would otherwise bind us.

The outcome of this mutual empowerment is freedom—the freedom we need to achieve a higher level of service and fulfillment. When we realize that we have our own place in this world, we will exchange thoughts freely, be better understood, enjoy enriching connections with others, and experience the exponential growth that is fostered by empowering relationships.

In this environment of freedom, we can embrace each other's visions and encourage one another to articulate the future we foresee. We will find ourselves and our purposes clarified and our values illuminated. We will benefit from the dynamics of mutual feedback and accountability. Each of us will enjoy the experience of seeing our dreams come alive and our unique contributions intermingled to make a difference in the world.

You are brilliant by birth. No one can fill your shoes, but others are poised to come alongside, and still others are waiting to follow in your footsteps—to freedom.

It's Your Life—Frame It!

In my coaching office, I have an ornate picture frame with no picture in it. I'm sure it is perplexing to those who enter my office for the first time, although at some point, each client learns what the mysterious wall-hanging is all about.

Naturally, because of my work in Hollywood, I can relate the empty frame to the way a film scene is conceived, visually speaking. As the director develops the look of the movie, he or she imagines the framing of each shot and decides how to accomplish the desired onscreen effect. (You may have seen documentary footage of someone on a film or photographic set creating a frame with his or her fingers and moving the improvised frame around so as to visualize how the actual composition will look.)

My empty picture frame hints at directing of another sort—it makes the point that we are the directors of our own lives. Because the frame is empty, we get to choose which picture will go inside. We can make any decisions we want in order to achieve the desired composition; we can choose a different way, an alternative thought, a new perspective, another outcome. It's all about what *we want*, because as beautiful as the frame may be, it has no power to decide what goes inside it.

Now, the empty frame has been placed in your hands, the hands of a strong person standing and an absolute wonder of a person. The frame is yours to fill; the future is yours to envision, and you get to decide how it will look.

So, what will your life, your dreams, and the *you* that is emerging look like?

ENDNOTES

Preface

1. http://www.quotationspage.com/quotes/Eleanor_Roosevelt/ (accessed April 13, 2008).

Chapter 1: The Hiding Place

1. Hiroo Onoda, *No Surrender* (Annapolis, MD: U.S. Naval Institute Press, 1999).

Chapter 2: Check Your Gait

1. Gait. Merriam-Webster Online. http://mw1.m-w.com/dictionary/gait.

Chapter 3: Caught on Tape

1. Arrest. Dictionary.com. *Dictionary.com Unabridged (v 1.1)*. Random House, Inc. http://dictionary.reference.com/browse/arrest (accessed: April 13, 2008).

2. http://www.quotationspage.com/quotes/Dee_Hock/ (accessed April 13, 2008).

Chapter 4: Shatter Your Invisible Wheelchair

1. http://www.quotationspage.com/quotes/Franklin_D._Roosevelt/ (accessed April 13, 2008).

Chapter 5: Unmask Your Authentic Identity

1. Galatians 5:9.

2. Gershen Kaufman and Lev Raphael, *Dynamics of Power* (Rochester, VT: Schenkman Books, 1983, 1991), xiii, xiv.

3. Gershen Kaufman, *The Psychology of Shame* (New York, NY: Springer Publishing, 2004), 22.

4. Ibid, 7.

5. Gershen Kaufman and Lev Raphael, *Dynamics of Power* (Rochester, NY: Schenkman Books, 1983, 1991), ix.

6. Gershen Kaufman, *The Psychology of Shame* (New York, NY: Springer Publishing, 2004), 18.

Chapter 6: Choice—The Power of Your C.A.R.

1. http://www.quotationspage.com/quotes/Albert_Einstein/31 (accessed April 13, 2008).

2. http://www.quotationspage.com/quotes/Theodore_Roosevelt/(accessed April 13, 2008).

Chapter 7: Action Puts Your C.A.R. in Motion

1. http://www.quotationspage.com/subjects/actions (accessed April 13, 2008).

2. http://pawprints.kashalinka.com/anecdotes/astaire.shtml (accessed April 13, 2008).

3. http://pawprints.kashalinka.com/anecdotes/astaire.shtml (accessed April 13, 2008).

4. http://www.quotationspage.com/quotes/Ralph_Waldo_Emerson/ (accessed April 13, 2008).

5. Theodore Roosevelt, "The Strenuous Life" http://www.theodoreroosevelt.org/research/speech%20strenuous.htm (accessed April 13, 2008).

Chapter 8: Ride Your C.A.R. to Rewarding Results

1. http://www.thomasedison.com/edquote.htm (accessed April 13, 2008).

2. http://www.quotationspage.com/quotes/George_Bernard_Shaw/ (accessed April 13, 2008).

Chapter 9: Take the Edge—Launch Your Biggest Life!

1. http://www.quotationspage.com/quotes/Anais_Nin/ (accessed April 13, 2008).

2. http://www.quotationspage.com/subjects/risk/(accessed April 13, 2008).

3. http://www.quoteworld.org/quotes/7814 (accessed April 13, 2008).

4. http://www.brainyquote.com/quotes/quotes/m/martinluth121065.html (accessed April 13, 2008).

Chapter 10: Experience Transformation: From Invisible to Transparent

1. http://www.quoteland.com/topic.asp?CATEGORY_ID=15 (accessed April 13, 2008).

2. Invisible. Dictionary.com. *Dictionary.com Unabridged (v 1.1)*. Random House, Inc. http://dictionary.reference.com/browse/invisible (accessed: March 26, 2008).

3. Wikipedia contributors, "Wonder Woman," *Wikipedia, The Free Encyclopedia,* http://en.wikipedia.org/w/index.php?title=Wonder_Woman&oldid=205257226 (accessed March 26, 2008).

4. Transparent. Dictionary.com. *Dictionary.com Unabridged (v 1.1)*. Random House, Inc. http://dictionary.reference.com/browse/transparent (accessed: March 26, 2008).

Chapter 11: Reframe Your Foundation in 10 Dynamic Days: Days 1–5

1. James 4:2 (NASB).

2. http://www.quoteland.com/topic.asp?CATEGORY_ID=61 (accessed April 1, 2008).

3. Champion. Dictionary.com. *The American Heritage® Dictionary of the English Language, Fourth Edition*. Houghton Mifflin Company, 2004. http://dictionary.reference.com/browse/champion (accessed: April 02, 2008).

Chapter 12: Reframe Your Foundation in 10 Dynamic Days: Days 6-10

1. http://www.quoteland.com/author.asp?AUTHOR_ID=138 (accessed April 5, 2008).

2. Arbiter. Dictionary.com. *Dictionary.com Unabridged (v 1.1)*. Random House, Inc. http://dictionary.reference.com/browse/arbiter (accessed: April 05, 2008).

Conclusion: You Are an Absolute Wonder!

1. http://www.quotationspage.com/quotes/Eleanor_Roosevelt (accessed April 7, 2008).

2. http://www.brainyquote.com/quotes/authors/e/eleanor_roosevelt.html (accessed April 7, 2008).

3. http://www.quoteland.com/topic.asp?CATEGORY_ID=255 (accessed April 8, 2008).

NOTES

ABOUT THE AUTHOR

To contact Terri visit www.TERRICADIENTE.COM

Terri proudly contributes to the following organizations:

Soroptimist International of the America's—improving the lives of women and girls locally and globally. Each book sold will send a donation to Soroptimists.

Soroptimist Live Your Dream Campaign —focuses on raising awareness about the unique challenges women face and ways that they can be supported in their quest to live their dreams.

Stuntwomen's Foundation —assists stuntwomen who, due to the nature of the business, have suffered injury and can no longer work.

Ragdoll Restoration Foundation—committed to raising the bar for girls ages 8 to17 with a parent in prison and the victims of human sex trafficking. "While we may not be able to take you out of your environment, we can offer you something to change the atmosphere." *–Terri Cadiente*

Mark Chironna Ministries—Each book sold will send a donation to MCM.

Additional copies of this book and other
book titles from DESTINY IMAGE are
available at your local bookstore.

Call toll-free: 1-800-722-6774.

Send a request for a catalog to:

Destiny Image₍ᵣ₎ Publishers, Inc.
P.O. Box 310
Shippensburg, PA 17257-0310

*"Speaking to the Purposes of God for This
Generation and for the Generations to Come."*

**For a complete list of our titles,
visit us at www.destinyimage.com.**